T17974

THE 100 GREATEST SPORTS BLUNDERS OF ALL TIME

ELDON L. HAM

D1417335

MASTERS PRESS

A Division of Howard W. Sams & Company

Published by Masters Press
A Division of Howard W. Sams & Company
2647 Waterfront Pkwy. E. Drive
Indianapolis, IN 46214

Printed in the United States of America.

97 98 99 00 01   10 9 8 7 6 5 4 3 2 1

Library of Congress Cataloging-in-Publication Data
Ham, Eldon L., 1952-
The 100 greatest sports blunders of all time / Eldon L. Ham.
          p.   cm.
ISBN 1-57028-159-9 (pbk.)
1. Sports-- United States-- Miscellanea. 2. Sports--United States--
History. I. Title.
GV583.H35   1997   97-37311
796'.0973--dc21   CIP

To my great friends and family, who deftly tolerate my own blunders with surprising regularity, and without whom I could not enjoy the fruits of life or pursue my private ambitions.

CREDITS:

Cover designed by Christy Pierce
Proofread by Pat Brady

ACKNOWLEDGEMENTS

Thank you's are difficult not for who is included, but for the deserving many who due to space and practicalities cannot be singled out. In particular, my many good friends and numerous family members (from Toulon to Glencoe and beyond) for whom I have dedicated my efforts know who they are and should never feel unappreciated.

Nonetheless, a few special mentions are in order, not the least of whom is Tom Bast who first believed in my work, and my editor Holly Kondras who helped him not regret it.

I would also like to thank my partner, friend and sounding board Steve Mandell for believing in me when I needed believing in; friends and dependable confidants Sally and Chris Gardocki; Chicago-Kent College of Law and associate dean Howard Chapman, first for accepting me as a student an unmentionable bunch of years ago, then for taking me on as an adjunct professor of sports law in 1995; Jack Kraft and Fred Fitzsimmons for being there when I and others needed them; Herb Young for encouraging my pursuit of sports law; and Jane Cheatham, my oldest friend whom I think of often but see too seldom.

Most of all, I am grateful beyond measure to my immediate family, not just for being there – after all, they have no choice – but for supporting and believing in each other, which is the way it should be: Mom and Dad ("Tibby" and John E., to most); wife, working mom and PTA president, Nan; Carla and Brandon; Jim Weiss; Gene and Sharyn; and most poignantly, Minerva, who regrettably never saw my manuscript, but who no doubt would have encouraged it – and me – anyway.

TABLE OF CONTENTS

THE 100 GREATEST SPORTS BLUNDERS OF ALL TIME

INTRODUCTION:
Of Mice, Men and Wally Pipp

Spectator sports are show biz. They sell drama, they sell glamour. But most of all they traffic in hope, conjuring up a means of identification for the vast majority of non-participants: we, the fans.

As the high school football team explodes through a marching band funnel blaring away at some oddly plagiarized fight song with frenetic cheerleaders in tow, the impending conflict is more than just entertainment for the student body, teachers and town folk. It offers a symbolic confirmation of belonging, hope and even self-justification. If the home team wins, we feel good about our team, our town, and most importantly ourselves. If Harvard beats Yale, the Harvard fans take pleasure. When the Chicago Bulls beat anyone, Chicagoans gloat.

Entertainment. Show Business. As the world of sports swells out over television airwaves, the stakes rise and the specter of big time sports takes root, marketing grandeur as never before. With the proliferation of professional franchises beyond New York and Chicago, penetrating the likes of Charlotte, Jacksonville, Portland and Salt Lake City, an eager public devours the hoopla with ravenous delight. If the home team fails, sophisticated fans are quick to critique, offering views, reviews and endless opinions on how to improve and win. It is little wonder sports talk radio has proliferated as a forum for the home crowd to cheer, mock, complain and offer endless tips on player trades, coaching and managing.

As teams and solitary gladiators such as boxers and tennis stars rise and fall, the analogy of sports to life begins to gel. With a contest life of only a few hours, and the life of an athlete's career extending just a handful of years, the evolution of "life" itself is dramatically compacted, exposing sports as a series of successes, mistakes, luck and shifting momentum where, it seems, sometimes nothing can go wrong or, regrettably, nothing can go right.

One of the mysteries of life, and one of the most compelling aspects of major sports endeavors, is the "Pogo" theory of failure, placing blame on the shoulders of those who would otherwise appear least deserving—ourselves. The succinct axiom, "We have met the enemy and the enemy is us," is a cruel, brutally honest philosophy of life which the world of sports has embraced to a fault. Nowhere is the aversion to success more noticeable than the environs of major league sports, an ironic bastion of war and winning with a curious penchant for snatching defeat from the proverbial jaws of victory.

Why do star players retire when they shouldn't, yet others shun retirement even though they should bow out gracefully at career's twilight? Football great Jim Brown retired at the peak of his career, probably too soon for his own good and certainly premature as the record books go; and Chicago Bull Michael Jordan did the same and realized, perhaps, that his time was not truly up and returned to the team after nearly a two season hiatus. Laker Magic Johnson, meanwhile, did a little of both. When he first learned of his HIV-positive status, Magic bailed out, probably too soon. When the fallout subsided and negative perceptions (his own included) waned, he was back—only to retire again in very short order.

Athletes, of course, are not the only perpetrators of questionable conduct. Fans perennially wonder aloud why recalcitrant owners break up their own dynasties, make trades of star players for no apparent cause, dump good coaches and hire bad ones, and then declare war on their own audience with lofty ticket prices and poor team products. A popular common sense rule "if it ain't broke don't fix it" is for some reason lost on owners, coaches and even athletes, with all of them scarcely missing a chance to tinker with the untinkerable or, worse, fiddle in Nero-like ignorance while the franchise goodwill billows its merry way up in smoke and ashes.

Sports blunders, if not a source of ironic inspiration, offer an entertaining look at the whimsical egos of those in control, or sometimes more aptly, those who crave an appearance of control. Often there is no viable explanation beyond just abject stupidity, but for some reason the cataclysmic blunders of sport are especially appealing, sometimes humorous examples of how life can go wrong when it is steered by the unwitting sports insiders in charge: themselves.

Intriguing as sports blunder are, one cannot fully plunge forward without some sense of definition, if not purpose. Yet the best beginning is to establish exactly what these faux pas are *not*. A reasonably cogent definition cannot include on-field playing errors, first because there are thousands of those each year and, secondly, athletic mistakes are largely a function of fate and, if genuine, are never planned. There has to be some foreseeable consequence that could have been avoided with a modicum of foresight, yet where the protagonist plods forward in spite of the apparent folly.

In this regard the great misfortune of one Wally Pipp, first baseman for the New York Yankees, misses the mark as a pure form of blunder. After winning three straight pennants alongside Babe Ruth from 1921 through 1923, one day in 1925 after an impressive eleven years with the Bronx Bombers, Mr. Pipp was stricken with a headache and requested a day off, a hiatus that was extended briefly when he was hit in the head by a practice ball soon thereafter. During his absence the Yankees found a replacement in newcomer Lou Gehrig who played the next 2,130 games in a row. Pipp was shipped out to the Cincinnati Reds where he finished an otherwise outstanding career which included three 90+ RBI seasons. Thus the erstwhile Wally Pipp may have experienced the height of bad luck, but it is difficult to saddle him with an otherwise avoidable blunder in the history of modern sports. Pipp, after all, had no way of knowing Gehrig's pending super stardom and, besides, his sickness was not planned—*and* perhaps his fate was unavoidable in any event.

Contrast Mr. Pipp's brief encounter with fate against the Boston Red

Sox folly of selling George Herman Ruth to the New York Yankees just as the incomparable Babe was charging toward baseball greatness and American sports destiny. This was a decision that not only had foreseeable dire consequences, it did not have to be made at all, heightening its apparent stupidity. But still further, the miscue had a profound impact not just on the owner who made it; rather, this error had profound repercussions for the Red Sox organization, the Yankees, the history of Major League Baseball, and the landscape of American sports and culture. What would the history of modern sports be without the "house that Ruth built" and Yankee dynasties piled—no, deliberately built—one upon another? This, then, is the essence of a sports blunder, a studied niche of historical significance qualified by a set of predetermined standards.

DEFINING THE SPORTS BLUNDER

A certifiable "sports blunder" is an intentional action with foreseeable consequences, affecting not just one athlete or event, but also with repercussions for a team, league or an entire sport. Here are the ground rules:

Impact on Sports

Stupid decisions by themselves don't count. There must be some profound or dire result, not just for the perpetrator, but somehow for sports in the larger sense. For example, even though Joe Namath's brash prediction of victory in Superbowl III may have been ill-advised, even stupid in the objective sense, Namath's Jets came through with a victory over the heavily favored Baltimore Colts. Opinions don't count, either. If they did, the hapless "New York Times" critic who in 1939 predicted sports could never make it on television would deserve a high ranking.

And to some measurable degree the results must be in. History may one day prove the gross folly of Shaquille O'Neal's move from Orlando to the Lakers—but at whose expense? Did the Lakers overpay for a brick-throwing monolith, or did Orlando quash its championship hopes for years to come? Either answer could one day complete the "blunder in progress," but so far Shaq's bolting fails to qualify for the list.

Reasonable Consensus

The event must be reasonably apparent in its folly. The use of Astroturf, for example, might be the bane of knees, legs and elbows of pro athletes, but others will point out its benefits to fans, players and the game by making domed stadiums possible, eliminating the fortuitous influence of weather and its elements. Likewise, those in Brooklyn would list the Dodgers' exodus as a disaster, but Los Angeles would argue otherwise.

Foreseeable Consequences

This relates back to the Wally Pipp syndrome: unfortunate, but not very predictable. All teams who passed upon third round pick Joe Montana made major mistakes, but they don't qualify as blunders because Joe was "a sleeper" that many people could and did miss. The same principle applies to the Celtics' draft pick Len Bias who died suddenly before he could make a contribution to the franchise. By contrast, Babe Ruth and Michael Jordan were obvious stars in the making when they were shunned by the Red Sox and Portland Trail Blazers, respectively. Perhaps no one could have predicted their ultimate levels of greatness, but those who missed out clearly had only themselves to blame.

Intent

The transgressor must intend the event and some (but not necessarily all) of its consequences. This precludes virtually all genuine playing errors, of which there are many, which influenced games, entire World Series, boxing championships and all the rest. Further, the decision or event must be made or intended within the context of sports: Although it's a close call, we presume the decision of the U.S. government to prosecute Muhammad Ali for alleged draft evasion was not intended to directly affect the sport of boxing, although it certainly did have a negative impact anyway; therefore, the government probably did not commit a "sports blunder" in the literal sense. However, the action of boxing authorities in removing Ali's license and title *was* sports related, unnecessary, and *did* change the course of professional boxing, not to mention the life of Ali himself—hence this portion of Ali's remarkable odyssey does make our list.

Contrast the government's action toward Ali with another government faux pas when the U.S. Supreme Court opined that Major League Baseball is not a business in interstate commerce, thus exempting Baseball from anti-trust laws and changing the course of American sports forever. Just as the transgressions against Ali narrowly miss, the Supreme Court's boneheaded blunder narrowly qualifies for it apparently *was* aimed solely at influencing the business of Baseball. Its repercussions are so profound, widespread and long lasting that this government blunder receives considerable attention and an anointed position atop the all-time blunder list.

Accountability

The bad move or decision must be somewhat traceable to a single source for purposes of the blunder rankings. The fact that black Americans were denied the participation in major sports for decades certainly impacted sports history, but this was not a foolish event or decision traceable to a single transgressor or committee (although Baseball's original commissioner Judge Kennesaw Mountain Landis had much to do with it). (For analogous reasons, a half-century of NCAA enforced stupidity also will not be found on the all-time blunder list.) However, one *will* find Adolph Hitler's bizarre 1936 Olympics and his related challenge to African American Jesse Owens, for Owens' profound success was a back-handed blunder by Hitler that did set the stage for black athletes in the decades to come.

With these parameters in mind, here is one version of the one hundred all-time dumbest sports decisions, duds and blunders influencing sports as we know them today. As a preliminary footnote, the reader will discover two athletes (Michael Jordon and Kareem Abdul-Jabbar) appear twice each reflecting, if not honoring, their super stardom. However, as either the perpetrator or target of no less than five top-100 blunders, it is the one and only Muhammad Ali who once again surfaces as "the greatest" for his relentless impact upon the great American sports adventure.

CHAPTER ONE:
We Have Met the Enemy...

...and the enemy is "us," of course. This axiom of life attributable to the cartoon pundit Pogo could very well kick off every chapter, if not every single sports blunder from 1 to 100. Starting in reverse order, the bottom ten blunders are dominated by athlete miscues and miscalculations. The Olympics are well represented in this bottom group, with one entry each from the summer (track star Ben Johnson, #99) and winter Olympics (notorious figure skater Tonya Harding, #100). And Pete Rose's gambling odyssey gets considerable play with two monster blunders in one.

Curiously, four of these first ten miscues involve Chicago sports in some manner, probably for three chief reasons. First, the author is from Chicago and has kept a close eye on the Chicago "dumb-o-meter" for many years; Chicago sports have been around for a relatively long period accumulating much good and bad history with several of the franchises (Bears, Cubs and Sox) among the oldest in their respective leagues; and, third, Chicago teams have indeed demonstrated remarkable historical acumen for bungling on and off the field.

Ranking any given blunder is wide open to interpretation, if not criticism, but the overall relative rankings should evoke less controversy. Keeping the objective blunder definition and rules in mind, it is always debatable whether to rank a given action at number 90 as opposed to 91 or 89. But if one loosely interprets the relative rankings as being in the bottom fourth, the

9

top fourth, and so on, then a degree of order and continuity should present itself. For example, the Cubs losing star player Lou Brock in a lopsided 1960's trade (blunder #97) is clearly less significant than Portland passing up Michael Jordan in the NBA draft (#4). Whether the Red Sox selling Babe Ruth (#3) is a bigger mistake than the Portland-Jordan blunder is fuel for great debate, but the author elected to give the Ruth deal more weight based upon a longer measure of historical impact, the breadth of that impact, and the probability that based upon information available at the time, the Ruth move was somewhat more dim-witted than the more recent Jordan "non-move."

Relative placement can depend upon stupidity, the result, and the overall impact upon sports. In other words, a large blunder with relatively small impact may rank lower than a more understandable mistake which, though smallish, may undermine a profound segment of American sports history. Incredible stupidity, though, will get high marks where justifiable, leading us to the first of our 100 blunderers, Tonya Harding.

The Tonya Harding Misadventure

Whether actively or passively involved—her own accounts are vague at best—Tonya's misadventures in the arrogant assault upon rival figure skater Nancy Kerrigan were an extraordinary blunder for Harding's sports career. Although her personal celebrity status temporarily increased (predicated upon infamy rather than admiration), her heightened name recognition was (and still is) the function of a national joke. The assault did not eliminate Kerrigan from the 1994 Olympics and failed to elevate Harding to a higher plateau, but it did arguably contribute to Kerrigan's silver medal finish instead of first place gold. It certainly altered world figure skating for the better part of a year, and the fallout still hangs over a sport where intense rivalries at all levels have become the butt of growing criticism, especially concerning youngsters and their sometimes overly enthusiastic, even abusive parents.

To add insult upon literal injury, a home-court judge in Harding's own community made a professional fool of himself and protracted the sports blunder by failing to support Tonya's removal from the U.S. Olympic team when she sued to enjoin the U.S. Figure Skating Association from revoking her credentials. The USFA had dropped her qualified status and provided for an internal hearing at which Harding could defend herself, but the judge ruled that she did not have adequate time to prepare for the hearing in view of the fast approaching Olympics. He failed to recognize that the approaching Olympics were the focus of the scheme

Tonya Harding's quest for gold fails to pan out.

itself—if the Olympics had not been just around the corner, the assault would not have been implemented—and thus rewarded the perpetrators by pushing the hearing to after the Olympic competition. The judge ignored well-settled law on the subject of interfering with internal actions of private associations such as the USFA and Olympic Committee: the usual requirements include a showing of bias or prejudice and the failure to provide notice and a hearing. Although the USFA was clean on all counts, the presiding judge recklessly took full advantage of his judicial prerogative to elevate foolish form over substance, effectively eliminating an otherwise deserving team member to make room for Harding and rudely altering the course of the 1994 Olympic figure skating competition.

The sheer stupidity and selfishness of the attack assure it a place on the all-time blunder list, which it barely makes at slot #100; but it fails to rank higher only because it may not have knocked Kerrigan out of first place—perhaps the competition did that, notably Oksana Baiul—and in any event its long-term effect upon the Olympics or upon the sport of figure skating is speculative. Nevertheless, it did have quite an effect upon the 1994 Olympics in full view of the world as Tonya struggled through her ill-fated performance as a tainted member of the U.S. Olympic team, leaving a global impression that is unlikely to wane soon.

11

Ultimately Harding plea bargained a deal with Portland authorities pursuant to a criminal investigation of the ordeal. She accepted three years' probation, $150,000 in fines and 500 hours of community service. She was also saddled with a Class C felony conviction, removable after three years if she exhibits the appropriate good behavior.

One footnote to the Harding-Kerrigan Olympics: Figure skating scores are somewhat biased, not necessarily reflecting the cumulative intent of all the judges. Even given the exact scores earned at the 1994 Olympics, had the judges utilized ranking methods devised by the French mathematician J. C. Borda in 1770, Kerrigan would have beaten Oksana Baiul. The ranking system actually used emphasizes first place votes, but some suggest it does not sufficiently penalize a skater for especially low marks. In 1994, Baiul was ranked first by five judges, second by two, and third by two. Kerrigan received four firsts, five seconds and *no* third place votes. In the Borda system, Kerrigan's one less first place would be more than made up by Baiul's two third place slots—hence Kerrigan would have won.

Ben Johnson's Steroid Olympics

The Seoul Summer Olympics of 1988 produced drama, excitement and stunning performances as Florence Griffith-Joyner burst to a new world record of 21.34 seconds in the 200-meter finals, the East German swimmer Kristin Otto captured six gold medals in swimming, and American swimmer Matt Biondi won five golds, a silver and a bronze medal. But one of the greatest Olympic feats of 1988 transformed defeat to victory for track legend Carl Lewis who was awarded the gold medal for the exalted 100-meter dash.

Canadian track star Ben Johnson, muscles rippling with power, exploded to a new 100-meter world record of 9.79 seconds only to be stripped of both his gold medal and the record three days later when he tested positive for illicit performance enhancing drugs. Johnson's resort to the enhancers was undoubtedly a blunder, one which would drift into relative obscurity but for his stunning record time, the focus he brought upon athletic drug use, and the profound effect his disqualification had on the one and only Carl Lewis. At the Los Angeles games of 1984, Carl Lewis paid homage to icon Jesse Owens by winning four golds in the track and field competition. He claimed gold in each of the 100-meter dash, the 200, the 4 x 100 relay and the long jump. Although Johnson blew by Lewis in the 100 four years later, Johnson's disqualification for drug use launched Lewis into gold again, helping maintain a string of gold victories of "Olympic" proportions themselves. Four years hence at the 1992 Barcelona games, Lewis would find a way to take Olympic gold in the long jump, besting fellow American and world record holder Mike Powell.

Although performance enhancing drugs had crept into Olympic awareness before via weightlifters, female track stars and others, Ben Johnson's dramatic fall from grace in the visible 100 meters profoundly captured the attention of a shocked world audience, leaving behind a tarnished Olympic image and a bittersweet victory for the great Carl Lewis.

The Pete Rose Odyssey

"The trouble with baseball today is that most
of the players are in the game for the money."
—Ty Cobb, 1925

There is a gaping hole in the Major League Baseball Hall of Fame because of a series of mistakes that led to and aggravated the professional demise of Baseball's all-time hit leader and unofficial "Charlie Hustle," Pete Rose. His gambling escapades, income tax evasion, and related legal warfare with commissioner Bart Giamatti combined to assure his profound fall from grace, begging a lingering controversy about whether Rose should be in the hall of fame regardless.

In 1985 Pete Rose passed Ty Cobb's major league record 4,191 career hits, eventually amassing 4,256 total hits from his "rookie of the year" debut in 1963 through his retirement as a player in 1987. Notwithstanding Rose's

Pete Rose struck himself out against Major League Baseball. (Photo by Terry Bochatey, UPI/Corbis-Bettmann)

extraordinary accomplishments, Commissioner Giamatti set out to ban Rose from Baseball, forever denying his ability to manage, own, scout or otherwise be affiliated with the sport. As fate would have it, Rose's blunders were mostly self-inflicted and magnified by a strategic decision by his lawyers in challenging the Giamatti action.

With the legacy of a gruff, tough Kennesaw Mountain Landis as Baseball's first and most powerful commissioner, Major League Baseball has a history of strong independent commissioners (until now—see the Bud Selig fiasco at item #27). The few limitations on their powers include a prohibition against pre-judging cases and controversies before them, a restriction imposed also by customary legal principles (see Tonya Harding at #100). Commissioner Giamatti deftly invoked his sovereign powers, but he overplayed his hand with Pete Rose.

Remarkably, Rose and his lawyers caught Giamatti violating his legal duty when they turned up a "smoking gun" letter written by the commissioner while Rose's gambling case was still before him. Purportedly before Giamatti had heard the whole case on the gambling charges, the commissioner had sent a supportive letter to a "snitch" witness who had testified against Rose, thanking the witness for testimony that Giamatti described in writing as "candid, forthright and truthful." But Giamatti could only have described the testimony as truthful if he *believed* it, and that meant he had prejudged the case! Rose had the goods on the commissioner—cold. But then he blundered yet again, this time suddenly dropping his case in an abrupt settlement whereby Rose would not contest the commissioner's power or his right to suspend him, provided that Rose would never have to admit the gambling episodes.

This decision was possibly made to avoid negative testimony that might hurt Rose's pending tax evasion case with the IRS, but it—and particularly its timing—was especially unfortunate because within a matter of days after the settlement, Giamatti abruptly dropped dead of a heart attack! Had Rose stuck it out just a brief while longer, the Giamatti smoking gun letter would have survived Giamatti himself, thrusting Rose back into the legal driver's seat. However, that was not to be, with fate exiling infielder Rose to "left field," forever altering the historical landscape of major League Baseball, its record books and the hall of fame.

The Rose debacle receives high marks for stupidity, especially the gambling scandal and all that went with it, but it does not rank higher because Rose was already retired by the time he was banned. Of course under the terms of the suspension he will never manage again, which has a continuing impact, but the playing records remain unaltered, as does his overall career on the field. Had these mishaps occurred during his playing days, the results would be much more damaging to Baseball itself (see Denny McLain at #76).

As it is Baseball is simply left with a tarnished record book, ignoring Rose's Hall of Fame stature. Pretending a player does not exist is not the proper response. Why not put Rose in the Hall, but disclose the full truth— good and bad? Otherwise the record books look absurd. The official National League "Green Book" (1995) for example, lists the top ten players in National League history in various career categories, and in each of these seven categories Rose is expressly labeled as the *only* player not in the Hall of Fame: Games Played; Total Singles; Total Bases; At Bats; Doubles; Runs

Scored; Hits. And Rose ranks number 1 in six of those seven! He bests the likes of Willie Mays, Hank Aaron, Lou Brock, Honus Wagner, Ernie Banks and Stan Musial in every category that Rose appears in, except total bases where he is "only" fourth with 5,752 behind monster home run sluggers (Aaron—6,591 total bases; Musial—6,134; and Mays—6,066). Each member of these all-time lists carries an asterisk designating Hall of Fame status—except Rose. (His quirky *lack* of an asterisk is an ironic juxtaposition to Roger Maris' plight of having the *only* asterisk for his own single season home run record.)

"Bull" Durham's Wet Glove

The hapless Cubs made two serious runs at the World Series in the 1980's, falling short in both 1984 and again in 1989.

The '84 team was an awesome collection of hitters and pitchers, coming within one game—perhaps even one single play—of the elusive World Series. With a two game lead in a five game league championship series against the San Diego Padres, the Cubs blew game three and collapsed in the series with three straight losses.

The Cubs opened the San Diego series at home with Rick Sutcliffe on the mound, a lofty (6'7") overpowering right hander who could hit, banging out a homer himself in game 1. In all the Cubs knocked five dingers among Sutcliffe, Bob Dernier, Ron Cey and Gary (the "Sarge") Matthews who hit two as they blew out the Padres 13-0. In game two, the Cubs won again behind the tall (6'4"), quirky, left hander Steve Trout, this time doubling the Padres up with a 4-2 score.

With just one victory to go, the Cubs stumbled in San Diego, losing 7-1 even though they had trotted out one of the most effective and durable pitchers in recent history, Dennis Eckersley. Game four was a nail biter tied at 5-all in the bottom of the ninth when Steve Garvey (four for five on the day) blasted a two-out home run with Tony Gwynn on base and suddenly the series was tied at two games each.

To win the pennant, the Padres would have to become the first National

League team to overcome a two game deficit—*and* they would have to beat the invincible Rick Sutcliffe doing it. The Cubs got off to a fast 3-0 start after two innings and Sutcliffe was cruising, giving up just two infield singles in five innings. After six, the Cubs were still clinging to a 1-run lead when the wheels came off. In the bottom of the seventh inning a walk and sacrifice put the tying run on second base. With one out, a Padres pinch hitter hit a grounder that rolled beyond the mit and through the legs of first baseman Leon "Bull" Durham, allowing the tying run to score. An "excuse me" check swing hit to left followed, then Tony Gwynn punched a tricky one-hopper over the shoulder of National League MVP Ryne Sandberg scoring two more runs. One more single padded the Padres lead to 6-3 and the late-inning carnage sparked by Durham's error was complete, knocking the Cubs out of the World Series and ushering in the San Diego Padres.

Since on-field playing errors do not "officially" qualify for sports blunder recognition, Durham's ground ball error would otherwise dribble into obscurity. But it receives special attention because Cub lore (the Cubs have "lore"; the Yankees, for example, have "history," a mild distinction with a big difference) finds a vial of liquid being kicked over onto Durham's mitt *off* the field, soaking it in something stickier than water — maybe juice or even GatorAde — and then Durham elected to use the mitt in the game anyway. Could this nondescript club house blunder have kept the Cubs from the World Series? Perhaps. As in all sports events, it is usually unfair, if not inaccurate, to blame team losses on one person or a single miscue; but an argument can be made that the momentum stirred by Durham's lapse in judgment tipped the final game of the final series of the Cubs' near miss of 1984.

73 to 0!

The Chicago Bears won the 1940 NFL championship game by the astonishing score of 73-zip, thoroughly trouncing an excellent Washington Redskins team by a margin of victory unlikely to be surpassed in any major championship contest in any pro sports league. Although the on-field mistakes that led to such a slaughter must have been frequent, what was all the fuss to qualify the 1940 championship for top-100 consideration?

First, the Redskins-Bears rivalry was intense. Washington defeated Chicago 28-21 to capture the 1937 championship, and the following year the Bears won a regular season encounter 31-7. The teams did not meet in 1939, but in 1940 the Bears lost a low scoring league game to the Redskins by a 7-3 margin. The legendary George Halas, who virtually founded the NFL itself, was the Bears' coach throughout this period. After the narrow 7-3 loss, Halas complained about the Redskins, the officiating and whatever else he could muster, and Redskins coach George Preston Marshall jumped all over Halas' protestations, reportedly announcing that "the Bears are a bunch of crybabies." Undaunted, he went on, "They are a first-half club. They are quitters. They are the world's greatest crybabies."

Taunting. It is a ploy that backfires more often than it inspires one's own troops. For example, it is widely understood that a taunted Michael Jordan is always at his most dangerous. And taunting a good Bears team with public insults upon the injury of scoring just 3 points in their last Redskins game was like throwing burning matches at kerosene.

The Bears were still developing the T-formation, and the coaches stayed up all night selecting plays for the championship game. In an effort to outdo himself, George Marshall could not resist one more trip to the well, taunting the Bears with a last minute telegram saying, in part:

"Congratulations. I hope I will have the pleasure of beating your ears off next Sunday and every year to come. Justice is triumphant. We should play for the championship every year."

Washington was led by the legendary passing quarterback Sammy Baugh, and the Bears had a punishing running attack bolstered by a bone crushing defense. Chicago came on strong, knocking the Skins back on their heels, but by half-time the score was still within reach at 28-0 Chicago. But on the very second play of the second half, Baugh laid one up which was picked off at the 15 and returned for a touchdown: 35-0. Skins ball again, fourth and 20 on their own 34 yard line. Baugh's pass falls incomplete and the Bears take over on downs. A quick opener, a gaping hole in the line, and the Bears are up 41-0 (the extra point failed). Another interception: 48-0. And another: 54-0. It was still the third quarter.

As the fourth quarter began, a frustrated Skins player punched out a Bear for a 15 yard penalty, followed by a Bear quarterback reverse and a touchdown: 60-0. After a fumble recovery the Bears scored again on a 2 yard dive to take a 66-0 lead. The referee asked Halas not to kick for the extra point, for the officials had brought nine balls to the game and eight had already been lost in the stands on kicks. So the Bears passed for their conversion point: 67-0.

An interception, ten more Bear plays, and a touchdown brought the tally to 73-0 (the extra point failed). Every Bear player saw action in the game, ten of them scoring touchdowns. True to their reputation, the Bears had dominated the game on the ground and with defense. The Bears only passed the ball eight times all day, but they ran for 372 yards while holding the Redskins to a net 3 yards rushing for the entire game. Washington passed 49 times, with the Bears intercepting eight and running five back for touchdowns. The loud mouth George Marshall, who taunted the Bears indiscriminately, was now turning on his own players, calling them quitters.

While the press struggled for descriptive hyperbole from "massacre" to "Waterloo," the Bears' George Musso summed it up best: "We wanted revenge and we got it." George Marshall's antics, Bears intense preparation and game dominance, and a shell-shocked Washington team all added up to one thing—a major blunder born of ridicule and ending decisively with revenge. Never before has a big league pro championship been so lopsided—and perhaps none ever will.

Ryne Sandberg

Dallas Green was a mainstay of the Phillies baseball organization, even pitching for Philadelphia in the 1960's. Green, though, made a different mark for himself in the early 1980's rebuilding the Chicago Cubs as general manager. His inspiration was to emulate the successful Phillies ball club, even to the point of hiring former Phillies coach Lee Elia as field manager, then raiding Phillies personnel—all players that Green knew intimately. In 1980 he pirated Keith Moreland, and then in January of 1982 Green went after Philadelphia shortstop Larry Bowa. He gave up Ivan DeJesus and demanded a "throw-in" youngster to be included with Bowa. The Phillies obliged, kicking in 22-year-old minor league infielder Ryne Sandberg. The rest, they say, was history.

Sandberg was initially moved to third base in 1982 where he immediately set a Cubs record for steals as a third baseman. He also set a Cub rookie record for runs scored at 103, and was named to the Topps Major League All-Rookie Team. Moved to second base in 1983, Sandberg won a Gold Glove for fielding. In 1984, the year the Cubs took San Diego to a five game series for the National League pennant, Ryne Sandberg was a starter in the All-Star game and named National League MVP. In 1985 Sandberg became only the third major leaguer in history to have at least 25 home runs and 50 steals in the same season. The following year he set a National League record for fewest errors in a full season (5). Eventually he broke Manny Trillo's record of 89 consecutive errorless games played at second base. Notwithstanding a brief, ill-advised retirement, Sandberg was still starting for the Cubs in 1997, fifteen years after his rookie season.

Not all bad trades are blunders, of course, but some are too glaring to ignore. The Philadelphia failure to recognize what they had in Sandberg was a blunder all its own, and the throw-in trade deal was an extension of their mistake. Considering that Sandberg became a virtual major league star in the very year of his trade, 1982, it is difficult to imagine what the Phillies missed that Dallas Green saw clearly. Sandberg has proceeded to leave his unique mark on the Chicago Cubs and all of baseball, and it is no coincidence that the Cubs were inches away from the National League pennant in both 1984 and 1989 when Sandberg produced "career" years.

Cardinals Dump Rogers Hornsby

Slight of build but long on bravado, the soon-to-be-great Rogers Hornsby broke into the major leagues in 1915 with more of a whimper than a bang. The St. Louis Cardinals picked him up on a hunch and in 1916, his first full season, Hornsby grabbed baseball history by the throat and wouldn't let go for twenty-three years. In his first four complete seasons, Rogers batted .313, .327, .281 and .318 as an infielder playing mostly shortstop and third base. Vocal and brash, he immediately was one of the best hitters in the league—and he knew it.

By 1920 Hornsby was moved to second base where he would solidify his rightful perch in baseball history. Under the tutelage of the one and only Branch Rickey, Hornsby improved his strength and size, boosting his weight from his rookie year 140 pounds to a muscular 200. From 1921 to 1925, Rogers went on a tear winning the league batting title five straight years with performances of .397, .401, .384, .424 and .403—an overall 5-year average of .401! For good measure, Hornsby landed league home run titles in 1922 (42 homers) and 1925 (39); and his .424 average of 1924 is still the highest single season mark of the twentieth century.

By 1926 Hornsby's acerbic confidence caught up with him as old animosities surfaced with Cardinals owner Sam Breadon over Rogers' contract. Breadon ignored public sentiment and engineered a trade to New York, "dumping" Hornsby on the Giants' manager John McGraw. Fan reaction in St. Louis was almost violent as Breadon was shredded daily by the newspapers and the Chamber of Commerce threatened to back a boycott of the park. Now a Giant, Hornsby continued to flourish, hitting .361 in 1927 and leading the league in both games played and runs scored. In 1928 the Giants struggled and Rogers was traded to the Boston Braves where the Hornsby juggernaut kept rolling with a .387 average to lead the league for a seventh time. After 1928 Rogers was traded to the Cubs for five players and $200,000 in cash—a notable sum in those days. As player-manager, Hornsby led the Cubs to third place in 1931 with a .331 average and 90 RBIs, but by 1932

21

he was running out of steam and played in only 19 games.

Remarkably, Branch Rickey brought Hornsby back to the Cardinals in 1933 where he batted .325, after which he exited to manage the St. Louis Browns where he played occasionally and hit a cumulative .299 over five more seasons! Had Hornsby remained with the Cardinals throughout, he would have set Cardinal records galore (his lifetime average of .358 was second only to Ty Cobb). As it is he returned in 1933 anyway, and certainly the only real impediment to his tenure was the ego of Cardinals owner Sam Breadon, which cost St. Louis eleven more years of Hornsby's heroics. The gaff was even more absurd given that Hornsby had become part owner of the Cardinals during his first tenure—which all had to be unwound for a hefty sum when he was dumped by Breadon.

03 Roger Maris*

Yankee slugger Roger Maris maintains the Yankee, American League and Major League Baseball record for home runs in a season with 61. Icon Babe Ruth still owns three other Yankee non-pitching records for season high batting average (.393 in 1923), runs scored (177 in 1921) and walks (170 in 1923), but his 60 home run standard was eclipsed in 1961 by Roger Maris in a year when he and Mantle hit over 50 dingers apiece. But at the time, Babe Ruth's record was almost holy, a shrine of baseball's great golden era, and Maris was afforded near-pariah status for knocking Ruth from the top of the charts. Unable to cope with its new hero, Major League Baseball awarded Maris the most famous asterisk in sports history—arrogantly denying Maris' unqualified right to the top spot by denoting his record came at a time when the American League played more games than in Ruth's era.

This is the only time that Baseball singled out a player for such scorn, and it wore on Maris emotionally. Many Yankee records were set by various players after Maris' 1961 season, including a dubious mark for pitcher Ralph Terry in 1962 for most home runs allowed (40), plus a couple of single season pitching records from Ron Guidry in 1978 (most strikeouts—248; most shutouts—9), but no one has received the lukewarm accolades that Maris did. Compounding the Maris problem was a noticeable lack of charisma, especially when compared to his ebullient teammate Mickey Mantle. Most fans, in fact, probably rooted for Mantle to win the crown, so when both he *and* Ruth were overtaken by Maris they were disappointed twice.

But the unfairness of the "*" is symbolically profound, representing a dig at Maris and effectively keeping Ruth in the record books. An argument could be made for leaving Maris' plight off the blunder list, but its folly affects more than just Maris the man. It changed the way the ultimate baseball record was maintained for years, and represented a glitch in Yankee and Major League Baseball lore. One of the most compelling reasons to include it on the list, however, is its sheer "unnecessariness"—the folly, even the stupidity, of it all, tarnishing the Baseball record books (not to mention Maris) for no reason. The potential precedent was ridiculous, if not dangerous, for not long afterward Henry Aaron broke the other invincible Ruth mark for most home runs in a career (733). Should Mr. Aaron be demeaned by an asterisk? How about everyone else since 1961? Fortunately, the asterisk has since disappeared in the record books, with the official American League "Green Book" clearly listing Maris in first place for homers in a season.

92 Magic Johnson

In 1979 a youthful Earvin "Magic" Johnson was MVP of the NCAA final four, leading Michigan State to a national basketball championship over Larry Bird's second place Indiana State team. Sixteen years later, during the 1995-96 NBA season, a seasoned and much older Magic was struggling with a comeback after retiring four years earlier due to his HIV-positive health status. Magic rejoined the Lakers on January 30, 1996, and in 32 games averaged 14.6 points and 6.9 assists, becoming only the second player in NBA history to eclipse 10,000 career assists (Utah's John Stockton being the other).

Along the way, Johnson the warrior had led great Lakers teams of the 1980's, topping the NBA in assists four times, leading the league once in free throw percentage at a sizzling 91.1%, and being selected MVP of the all-star game twice (1990 and 1992). Although his records and championships are legendary, Magic's greatest trait was his versatility and leadership. A strong, speedy 6'9" with court awareness and stunning ball handling skills, Johnson had the talent to play any position from point guard to center. Although he made his mark as a point guard scoring and assist machine whose lightning passes sometimes bordered on the supernatural, Magic was once forced to play center during the playoffs as a result of injuries to Kareem Abdul-Jabbar, holding his own and leading the Lakers to victory.

If it is fair to saddle Ben Johnson with a sports blunder due to drugs, Pete Rose for gambling and other offenses, or Muhammad Ali for having one fight too many, can Magic's tragic HIV status be fairly criticized? Perhaps, since the events leading to his unfortunate health condition were his own doing; then again perhaps not, for few could foresee the dire consequences of indiscretion before it was too late. But Magic's lapses, coupled with an abrupt retirement and the painful indecision behind a four-year series of on-again off-again unretirements are worthy of mention not to condemn, but to honor Magic by recognizing his anguish, his personal loss and the loss of professional sports first by his grief, then by his absence. His premature loss to the NBA was profound, ceding the undisputed superstar crown to Michael Jordan, denying the Lakes their playmaker and spiritual leader, and robbing himself of a realistic shot at the NBA all-time assist record. Had Johnson averaged seven assists per game (a low guess) for four extra years, his career assist total could have exceeded 12,000 placing him neck-and-neck with John Stockton.

Not all sports blunders are without silver lining, however, and fate has made the most of Magic's plight. Johnson's exalted profile accelerated public HIV awareness, touching millions and jerking America forward in both its ability to accept the reality of AIDS and in its resolve to fight back—no small feat for any man, champion or not.

The Ghost of Lou Brock

According to the *Bill James Historical Baseball Abstract*, the most lop-sided baseball trade of the 1960's occurred when the Chicago Cubs shipped out Lou Brock (plus two others) for the likes of Ernie Broglio, Bobby Shantz and Doug Clemens.

Brock was a rookie in 1962 and was in good company playing alongside Cub greats Ernie Banks (37 home runs, 104 RBIs) and Billy Williams (22 homers, 91 RBIs). Brock himself showed stunning speed and hit for a decent average at .263. On June 27, 1962, Brock launched a mammoth home run 500 feet into the Polo Grounds' center-field bleachers against the expansion New York Mets, becoming only the second player in history to hit those elusive seats. Even so, the league Rookie of the Year was not Brock, but his teammate second baseman Ken Hubbs who hit .260 and set two major league records when he handled 418 chances over 78 straight games without an error. After the 1962 season, the Cubs and St. Louis Cardinals exchanged six total players in a trade that looked bad initially for the Cubs but proved a good one in hindsight.

The Cubs continued to build and improve. In 1964 Cub third baseman Ron Santo clubbed 30 home runs with 114 RBIs and a .313 average, tying the league lead in triples (13). He complemented icons Banks and Williams, the latter batting .312 with 33 homers and 98 RBIs, and the Cubs charged ahead through the middle 1960's with a fearsome long ball lineup. In the middle of the 1964 season, June 15 to be exact, the Cubs went searching for another pitcher. They found one in St. Louis by the name of Ernie Broglio, a powerful right hander who had won 18 games for St. Louis in 1963. Enamored with Broglio's arm, Cub management shipped Lou Brock out to the Cardinals in mid-season in a six-man deal that brought the erstwhile Ernie Broglio to Wrigley Field. Broglio immediately developed a sore arm and went bust, while Brock exploded onto the Cardinals scene batting .348 and rewriting every National League base stealing record in sight. He also led them to the World Series title in 1964 while the Cubs methodically racked up home runs in a brief run toward greatness that would fall short in 1969, the year of the miracle Mets.

The trade triggered a sparkling decade for perennial contender St. Louis, a stellar team for the record books sporting such stars as Bob Gibson, Curt Flood and the superstar speedster Brock while the rival Cub all-stars continued to fall short year after year. In 1969, one of the most notorious Cub teams in history exploded to a 10-game lead in August, then went into an unprecedented choke dive, succumbing to the Mets as the season drew to a close. Fielding a veritable National League all-star team with Ernie Banks, Ron Santo, Billy Williams, Glenn Beckert, Don Kessinger and Ferguson Jenkins, the 1969 Cubs rolled over all contenders with power and defense—but in hindsight fell short on speed and consistency. Without the Lou Brock trade blunder would the all-star Cardinals of the 1960's switched places with the all-star Cubs? Would the Cubs have won the World Series in 1969 instead of the Mets? Maybe.

With all of that, why not rank the Brock misadventure much higher? Initially it wasn't as dumb as history would later prove. In two full seasons as a Cub, Brock batted only .263 and .258, and in 1964 he was lower still at .251 on the eve of the trade. Further, in all honesty, Brock was not the number one star player of the Cubs (or even the Cardinals later, but he was close) and, finally, the effect of the trade blunder is sheer speculation—especially considering the sordid history of the Cubs who always find a way to lose regardless of who's in the lineup.

CHAPTER TWO:
Difficulties of Olympian Proportions

As the blunder countdown reaches 90, the next ten entries highlight the Olympics. Failed sex tests, a political suspension and a major gaff by the Paris Olympic games make their mark upon the sports landscape. And Butch Reynolds gets into the failed drug test act, filing suit and making a superb good case that the samples were mixed—plus winning a $27 million dollar judgment—demonstrating that not only are positive drug tests eligible for blunder consideration, but false positive tests can have repurcussions of international proportion.

Butch Reynolds

In 1992 Harry "Butch" Reynolds was a world class American amateur sprinter. He was also a world class plaintiff of sorts, suing the International Amateur Athletic Federation to enjoin disciplinary action stemming from a positive drug test indicating improper steroid use. He was at that time the world record holder in the 400 meters, an event in which Reynolds had won an Olympic silver medal at the 1988 Seoul games.

Reynolds had competed at an international track competition in Monte Carlo on August 12, 1990, after which he was randomly tested for illicit drugs. He was later notified he had tested positive, thus failing the test. Reynolds immediately went to Federal Court to enjoin a two year suspension

27

by the Federation, but was turned away for technical reasons since he had failed to first exhaust the private administrative remedies available to him through the U.S. Olympic committee and related amateur sport rules. So Reynolds voluntarily participated in an expedited arbitration proceeding on June 7, 1991, winning a decision three days later that cleared him to participate in the preliminary rounds of the World Championships beginning June 12, 1991.

In exonerating Reynolds from charges of steroid use, the arbitrator did not waver:

> The arbitrator finds that the Respondent's suspension of Mr. Reynolds was improper; that there is clear and convincing evidence that the "A" sample and the "B" sample did not emanate from the same person and the "B" sample did not confirm the "A" sample; that there is substantial evidence that neither the "A" sample or the "B" sample emanated from the Claimant [Reynolds]; and that the Claimant should be declared eligible to compete in the qualifying rounds for the World Game Championships..."

Undaunted, the Federation stubbornly refused to accept the result of the arbitration, insisting that the proceedings were not consistent with Federation procedures which empowered another regulatory body, The Athletics Congress (TAC), to handle post suspension disputes. This left Reynolds still ineligible, and so TAC scheduled another hearing for September 13, 1991. After two weeks of deliberation, the TAC hearing panel agreed with the first arbitration, specifically finding that the positive sample test had been impeached by clear and convincing evidence. Remarkably, even with these findings of TAC, the Federation *still* refused to reverse itself, instead invoking yet another rule to arbitrate the validity of the TAC decision. This time, after only two hours of deliberation, this third panel finally came to the opposite conclusion, finding "no doubt" as to Reynolds' guilt.

Butch Reynolds went straight back to Federal Court, this time having exhausted more than enough preliminary remedies, and obtained an injunction preventing the Federation from interfering with his ability to compete. In so ordering, the Court offered a glimpse of the gross deficiencies that led to Reynolds' positive test plus two independent arbitration panel findings that the results were a sham:

"...this Court believes—as did the American Arbitration Association arbitrator and the TAC hearing panel—that Reynolds has created a substantial doubt as to the accuracy of the reported results. Not only did Reynolds' expert testify as to numerous deficiencies in the [laboratory] testing procedure, he also testified as to several inconsistencies with the actual test results which make it highly unlikely that both samples actually originated with Mr. Reynolds. Finally, and perhaps most egregious of all, Plaintiff's expert testified that nondrolone is known to remain in an individual's body for a considerable period of time, and the fact that Reynold's urine allegedly tested positive for two metabolites of nandrolone on August 12, 1990, and tested negative for nandrolone one week later on August 19, 1990, casts considerable doubt on the validity of the August 12 test."

But the Butch Reynolds saga was far from over. An emergency appeal by the Federation reversed the findings, after which Justice Stevens of the U.S. Supreme Court reinstated the injunction with the full Supreme Court declining to reconsider Justice Stevens' order. Reynolds then ran the 400 meter Olympic trials in New Orleans, qualifying as an alternate on the U.S. Olympic 4x400 relay team, but the U.S. Olympic committee refused to allow him to travel to Barcelona for the games fearing reprisals from the Federation. After the Olympics a vindictive Federation extended Reynolds' suspension as punishment for his legal challenge to the bogus tests. In December of 1992, the Federal District Court entered a default damage award against the Federation of $27.3 million, including about $20 million in punitive damages.

There is little doubt that the Reynolds fiasco was a blunder of international proportions, proving again that the worst enemies are often ourselves. (As a side note, there are even published reports suggesting the breadth of the damage award was a chilling factor in the Olympic Committee handling of the Tonya Harding controversy and whether to appeal the Portland judge's finding that she should compete in the Olympics pending a full hearing on her involvement in the Nancy Kerrigan assault.)

Junior Bridgeman and Chris Dudley

Sometimes blunders receive high marks just for sheer stupidity, and often they are worthy of mention for their sweeping impact upon the sports world. The NBA saga of Junior Bridgeman and Chris Dudley contains some of the former and big doses of the latter, for the combined actions of these players virtually reinvented the NBA as it is today.

In 1987 Junior Bridgeman sued the NBA in a complicated antitrust action which produced a profound and far reaching settlement with the league, essentially creating in 1988 the foundation for the current salary cap in place by the NBA. Language was implemented to prevent players from circumventing the salary cap intentionally, preventing teams from entering into bogus sweetheart contracts just so they could be torn up at the opportune time to defeat the cap.

One rule that sparked a great deal of creativity, and still fosters much controversy, was the "veteran exception" to the salary cap limitations which allowed teams to re-sign their own veterans without going over the cap limits. This, as much as any other NBA provision, gives the ceiling its "soft cap" label, provoking a number of exceptions and inviting controversial agreements. In 1993 a number of NBA players, including Tony Kukoc of the Bulls and the Trail Blazers' Chris Dudley, inserted variations of an "out clause" into their long term team contracts giving them an ability to cancel each respective contract, effectively turning it into a one-year deal. Dudley, as a matter of fact, signed a seven-year deal for over $10 million with Portland, starting off with only the $790,000 available under the cap for the first year. Although Dudley could have gotten a better deal on the surface from other teams, his contract contained a valuable out clause, allowing him to play a year, then cancel and renegotiate for big dollars without going over the salary cap since he would then be a Portland veteran not subject to the cap dollar limits in existence since 1983 as a result of extensive negotiations with the players association.

The Dudley "one year and out" clause found its way into federal court with the NBA contesting its validity, arguing it was just an artificial means to circumvent an existing rule. A federal judge in New Jersey essentially agreed with the NBA, but the league lost anyway. The court believed that Dudley and others were circumventing the cap, but also observed that in totality the Dudley contract had no adverse effect upon the league as a whole, since before he signed with Portland he was in fact a veteran player with New Jersey capable of signing for big dollars under the Nets' cap exception. The court conceded that such reasoning would weaken the NBA cap objective if applied to all players, but a strict reading of the Junior Bridgeman settlement agreement did not mandate a finding to the contrary. Dudley had won.

That first year Chris Dudley broke his leg, but nonetheless he re-signed after his one year of service for a much improved $24 million over the next six years. The Bulls' power forward Horace Grant then bolted to Orlando under the auspices of this flexible new one-year provision, but upon resistance from the NBA the Magic, Grant and the league all settled upon a two-year clause. Since then, the NBA has implemented a more firm limitation, requiring veterans to play a prescribed length of time before qualifying as veterans outside the cap limitations. Nonetheless, the Bridgeman to Dudley contract sojourns coupled with the NBA foul-up in the Bridgeman settlement language, all served to create the current NBA salary cap landscape, profoundly shaping the destinies of teams and players. For example, for Michael Jordan to maintain his salary at fair market levels, the only team that can really sign him in the $30 million range without cap problems is the Bulls. For example, if Charles Barkley were to come to the Bulls at the close of his career, he might have to play at near the league minimum to gain a championship ring in Chicago. Likewise, the Bulls face perennial impediments in re-signing the likes of Dennis Rodman and in fact failed to keep newly acquired forward-center Brian Williams. Around the league, impedi-

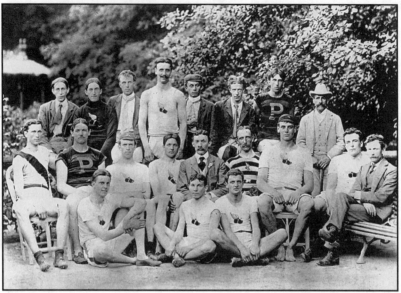

The U.S. Olympic team endured the 1900 Olympic follies. (Corbis-Bettmann)

ments have materially affected the movement and careers of Juwan Howard, Shaquille O'Neal, Alonzo Mourning and many others as the freedoms of free agency clash with the salary cap restrictions.

The Paris Olympics of 1900

The Olympic Games as we know them almost expired after the Paris games at the turn of the century.

The 1900 Olympics were a disorganized fiasco, so much so that most of the athletes competing didn't even realize they were in the Olympic Games at all! Paris was host to an international exposistion, essentially a world's fair, at exactly the same time, and for some inexplicable reason French officials saw the Olympics as a negative influence, dropping the term "Olympics" and just referring to the event as the "international championships."

It got worse from there: there was no cinder track, so sprinters ran on grass fields; hurdles were made of broken telephone poles; and discus throwers launched their throws into a shortened field, landing in the woods. Spectators stayed home, and often there were more athletes than anyone else. The marathon was run through a Parisian maze, and although the American world class favorite, Arthur Newton, took the lead and was never passed, he placed fifth behind a Swede and three Frenchmen including the "official" winner, a perfectly clean, dry bakery boy who apparently ran a much better, if not shorter (by about 25 miles) course en route to his wonderful "victory." But at least the marathon attempted to be a real event: other events included croquet, fishing and checkers.

The Olympics would undergo many more tribulations throughout the 20th century, including Hitler's 1936 games, the 1972 terrorist attack, and President Carter's boycott in 1980 (all three of which have also made the top blunder list), but it never again would experience pure indignities the magnitude of the 1900 games—and the Olympics as we know them were lucky to survive.

87 Failed Olympic Sex Test

The temptation of glory is great, hence any and every means to create an advantage has probably been tried at least once, if not often. One of the most sweeping and absurd gimmicks is "gender modification," a likely target since female contestants and records on the whole are less formidable than their male counterparts.

Any number of blunders are appropriate here, but the logical award goes to the first Olympic women's participant demonstrated to actually be, chemically speaking (or otherwise), a man, which goes to the erstwhile Polish runner Eva Klobukowska who failed a sex test in 1967 after having won a gold medal in a 1964 Olympic relay event, plus a bronze medal in the 100 meters. Eva may not have been the first who *should* have failed had the sex tests been administered earlier—simple logic suggests she probably was far from alone in her uniqueness—as Stella (Walsh) Walasiewicz who won gold and silver medals in the 1930's was observed to have "primary male characteristics" upon her death in 1980. Since sex testing at the Olympic Games themselves was not instigated until 1968 (probably inspired by Eva

Klobukowska's failure the year before in 1967), a number of dubious entries probably escaped detection. One most certainly would have been German high jumper, Dora Ratjen, who later was revealed to actually *be* a man in disguise at the 1936 Olympics. (Even so, it is interesting to note that he/she failed to medal, finishing only fourth.)

86 The Red Sox Squander Carlton Fisk

The 1996 official American League Red Book still lists the Red Sox darling catcher Carlton Fisk among the all-time Boston home run hitters in the company of Williams, Yastremski, Rice, Foxx, Petrocelli and Conigliaro. Fisk also graces the Red Sox all-time slugging percentage list, tied in ninth place at .481. Fisk's home runs as a catcher trailed only Yogi Berra and Johnny Bench in the history of the Major Leagues.

As American League Rookie of the Year in 1972, Fisk adorned the great Boston uniform and was a fixture at Fenway Park, catching and directing pitchers in the shadow of the famed "green monster" left field wall. Fisk himself was a New Englander in every sence of the word, having been born in Vermont and attending the University of New Hampshire. In 1974 Fisk missed much of the season with a broken collar bone, but in 1975 he hit .331 in 79 games in leading the Sox to the World Series. In game six of the Series Fisk leaped into baseball history with a stunning 12th inning home run to beat the Reds in game 6 in what many feel was the most dramatic game in World Series history. In 1977 Fisk hit .315 with 26 home runs, 102 RBIs and only four passed balls, and started the All-Star Game in both 1977 and 1978.

Injuries curtailed Fisk's performance the next two years, but even so in 1980 he hit .289 with 18 dingers. But as the Red Sox watched, the team perceived age catching up to Carlton Fisk and they became complacent, allowing Fisk to drift away in a most unusual fashion. In 1981 the Red Sox failed to postmark Fisk's new playing contract on time, causing him to become a free agent. Fisk shocked the team and all of Boston by signing with the Chicago White Sox and by 1985, thirteen years after his rookie season,

Fisk exploded for 37 home runs to lead the entire American League—an especially remarkable feat given the physical demands upon catchers and their inherently limited number of annual plate appearances, even allowing for extra pinch hitting or filling in as the DH.

Fisk's post-Boston days became so prolific that his second career in Chicago was better than his first. As of 1996, Carlton Fisk was still in the top ten on nine of twelve total White Sox hitting records, including seventh in all-time games played with 1,421, just short of Aparicio and Guillen, and ahead of Minnie Minoso. Not bad for an over-the-hill catcher, who also logged in first in home runs with 214 (but that was before Frank Thomas had a chance to catch up), fifth in RBIs (762), fifth in extra base hits (442) and sixth in total bases (2,143).

When the Red Sox failed to retain him, Fisk was not at the end of his career and he certainly was not an unknown quantity. Far from it—Carlton Fisk was an established star in his own right, a mainstay in his Boston uniform and a piece of major league history for his role in the fabled 1975 World Series which some enthusiasts have labeled one of the greatest ever. Yet after Boston's blunder he re-wrote the Chicago White Sox record books, leading them to an impressive 99-win season in 1983. Had Fisk remained with the Red Sox and, hypothetically, had he hit the same home runs there as he slugged in Chicago, his total Boston homers could have been 376, an enormous total for a catcher, which would have placed him ahead of Conigliaro, Petrocelli and even Foxx, and not far behind Carl Yastrzemski (452). More importantly, as a savvy catcher whose talent for working pitchers was legendary, Carlton Fisk's impact upon a team was immeasurable. History bears this out both during his Boston days and later with the White Sox when Chicago pitchers flourished during the 1983 division championship campaign.

Did his Boston exodus make a bigger impact than Lou Brock going to the Cardinals? Maybe. It is a judgment call, of course, but Brock wasn't so obvious a star when he eluded the Cubs. Although they should have recognized what they had in Brock, Lou was still developing and had not yet posted spectacular numbers for the Cubs when he slipped away. Was the

Fisk debacle more important than Tonya Harding's hooliganism? Probably. Less influential upon sports history than, for example, the Dempsey-Tunney long count? Perhaps not. More significant than the Rozelle Rule? No. The 1919 Chicago Black Sox? Absolutely not. But his departure for Chicago was a real, if not symbolic, example of the powers of free agency to "show up" team management, and Fisk's stay in Chicago padded the White Sox record books at the expense of Boston lore, and so his second career in Chicago was surely a blunder worthy of mention—especially considering the bungled manner in which Boston handled the presentation of his new contract. Even as a 40-year-old in 1988, Fisk was still going strong, hitting .277 with 19 home runs in just 76 games, batting still higher the following year at .293 with 13 homers.

85 Bears Sneaker Bowl

"I'll always believe *that* game was the key to the development of the NFL today," says Frank Gifford, Monday Night Football icon and former Giants star. According to a retrospective by the *Chicago Tribune's* Bill Jauss, Gifford was lauding the New York Giants-Chicago Bears sneaker bowl game of 1956 when Gifford's Giants smashed George Halas' Bears 47 to 7 in 18-degree bitter cold at Yankee stadium to win the NFL crown. The field was frozen solid, so the Giants tested new state-of-the art-sneakers obtained by one of their players a week earlier. In pre-game experiements, Giants defensive back Ed Hughes fell flat running with traditional cleats, but running back Gene Filipski didn't miss a beat.

Equipped with solid footing, Giants players like Sam Huff and Gifford ran circles around Bears stars J.C. Caroline and others. The night before an ice storm had blown through, and at game time it was still so cold the mustard at the hot dog stand froze. Why the big deal over the sneaker bowl? First, the Bears' shoes, even the non-cleated ones, had thinner soles and couldn't grip the turf like the Giants' shoes. Second, the NFL itself has echoed Gifford's sentiment, referring to the game as "among the most significant in NFL history" because it brought the glamour of pro football the attention of influential New York advertisers and showcased a Giants NFL title for an emerging television industry.

And just what were those magical sneakers? U.S. Keds.

Red Grange and the AFL

Legendary Bears coach George Halas founded the National Football League, but the "galloping ghost" Red Grange made it work, bringing style and distinction to his raggamuffin part-timers assembled to play football.

As a collective sweat poured from the brows of Fighting Illini fans on the sweltering 1924 season opener in Champaign, Illinois, the elusive Grange had scampered 95 yards for a touchdown on the opening kickoff against mighty Michigan. He wasn't through until he added four more impressive touchdown runs from scrimmage of 15, 45, 56 and 67 yards. The Ghost (a name coined by Grantland Rice) would nimbly maneuver around tacklers for 3,637 total yards at Illinois before signing a $100,000 per year guaranteed deal—a staggering sum given the times—to play for Halas' Bears. Grange and the Bears immediately drew 36,000 fans to Chicago's Wrigley Field for the Cardinals game on Thanksgiving day. Then the Bears traveled to New York and beat the Giants on a snow covered field before a paid gate of 65,000. Suddenly the National Football League was alive and kicking, a remarkable feat given initial public skepticism about how professional football would stack up against the extravaganza of big time college football: Notre Dame, Army, Yale, Michigan.

But Grange's opportunistic agent C.C. "Cash and Carry" Pyle read one too many press clippings and convinced Grange to quit the Bears and form an entirely new league, the first of three competing leagues to be christened the Amerian Football League. Grange played for a football team called, unoriginally, the New York Yankees and, although he did not get hurt financially, the new league itself was a major bust. Eventually his personal services contract with Pyle expired, Grange re-joined the Bears where he played for six more years before retiring in 1935. (Four years later the league began to emphasize the forward pass with Halas' radically new T-formation and his brash new quarterback from Columbia, Sid Luckman.)

Who knows what may have transpired had Grange not bolted the NFL for the folly of his own league? Could he have become part owner of the Bears—or of the league itself? What new records could he have set? The NFL would not see such an explosive, elusive runner until 30 years later in Gale Sayers, or maybe O.J. Simpson or Walter Payton, and given the crowds he drew perhaps Red Grange could have negotiated a lucrative incentive package tied to attendance. History will never know for sure, but Grange's exit from the Bears was a sports blunder that easily could have been avoided with an artful blend of logic and money.

83 Tommy Smith and the 1968 Olympics

The 1968 Olympics were not immune from the times, an era of war, protest, counter-culture, and racial strife in the wake of the King and Kennedy assassinations. It was not the first time politics would surface in the Games (note the Jesse Owens Oympics of 1936), and it certainly would not be the last (Munich in 1972; the boycotts by the U.S and then the Soviet Union), but 1968 would be a watershed Olympic year, ushering in a new kind of political venue for protest, free speech and world issues: the televised Olympics.

1968 was the year of the infamous Democratic National Convention in Chicago, the one where Mayor Daley's police became engulfed in riotous brutality against antiwar protestors gathered in and around Grant Park, the convention where Mayor Daley was the object of a campaign to unseat his Illinois convention delegation, the convention where Hubert H. Humphrey and the Democrats were so strongly identified with the volatile Vietnam War issue.

It is no wonder the summer games in Mexico grew into a forum for outrage and protest, as when Black American sprinters Tommie Smith and John Carlos placed first and third in the 200 meters. Moved by the domestic political strife of the times, Smith and Carlos took their places on the victory platform with symbolic defiance, black gloved fists raised steadfastly with their heads bowed in homage to human rights and black awareness, if not power. Although their visible world televised protestations were somewhat tempered, even benign when examined in historic context, both the U.S. Olympic Committee and the International Olympic Committee were highly offended at the time, citing Carlos and Smith for grossly unethical conduct before suspending and sending them home.

The Olympic committees achieved the exact opposite result than intended, of course. Smith and Carlos became martyrs, and their cases took center stage highlighting their protest even more as a grass roots groundswell for the "Olympic Project for Human Rights" (OPHR) took grip. The Cubans were among the first to show solidarity with their relay team sending its silver medals to the OPHR, and second place 200 meter winner Perter Norman from Australia had already worn the OPHR button when he was sandwiched between Smith and Carlos on the victory platform. According to published sources, a survey of twenty athletes on the U.S. team revealed thirteen in favor of the protest, five opposed. Combined with relentless Mexican student protests and a poignant level of success for African teams in general and those from Kenya in particular, the protest took on the dimensions of a world order political movement symbolizing, if not partly instigating, a shift in world political attitudes.

The Smith and Carlos protest was not the first injection of politics into the games by any stretch, and by itself lacked the immediacy of the 1956 Soviet invasion of Hungary which also stirred sweeping portest, but it did accomplish one result never before achieved: showcasing the Olympics on television as a powerful vehicle for international dissent. Was it a coincidence that four years later the infamous Israeli hostage crisis occurred at the Munich games? Or what about President Carter's boycott and the Soviet retaliatory boycott as the Olympics moved into the 1980's? One can only speculate, but we know for sure that the suspension was wholly unnecessary, tactically ill-advised and highly contrary to overall world opinion. In short, it was a needless, radical blunder potentially of world proportions.

First Failed Olympic Drug Test

Although sprinter Ben Johnson was one of the more famous athlete casualties of drug abuse, he was not the first and would not be the last. Interestingly, the first athlete to fail a test for performance enhancing drugs was probably a horse, since racehorces were tested as early as 1910. During the 1950's and 1960's anabolic steroids became popular among humans, especially weightlifters and football players impressed with the drug's ability to generate muscle mass. Use of anabolic steroids by high school athletes may have begun as early as 1959 when a Texas doctor allegedly administered Dianabol to members of a high school football team for an entire season.

Anabolic steroids are unique among enhancement drugs because they not only boost performance, they can alter an athlete's appearance. Users from professional wrestlers and bodybuilders to teenagers emulating macho images can achieve the "chiseled" look of muscled heroes by combining weight training with steroid consumption. When utilized in a program of weight resistance training, dietary modifications and caridiovascular training, steroids can have a profound effect on body size, strength and even speed.

Proper steroid use can be medically sound if used under a doctor's care for restorative purposes such as rebuilding damaged tissue. As such they are truly "restorative," helping to heal an athlete or non-athlete patient after injuries. Abuse occurs when "anabolic-androgenic" steroids become performance enhancers with athletes relying on them as additives, not to restore injured tissue, but to gain an unnatural athletic advantage. Not only is this unfair to the competition, and hence against the rules in virtually all legitimate sports, it poses extreme health hazards to the user. These steroids are synthetic derivatives of testosterone, the natural male hormone. The term "anabolic" means tissue building, while "androgenic" refers to the hormones' masculinizing traits. Steroid abuse has been associated with adverse effects on the liver, cardiovascular system, reproductive system and psychological health. In both men and women, there are increased risks of cancer, liver dysfunction, kidney disorders and heart disease.

But the will to win often outweighs the need for safety and fairness, so the temptation of steroid induced power and speed is sometimes difficult to resist. At the 1983 Pan American Games, 15 athletes from 10 countries (including the U.S.) were disqualified because of steroid use, causing three gold medals to be rescinded. In 1990, one thousand six hundred National Football League players received questionnaires about steroid use. Only 7.5% responded, but the indications from that limited group suggested that 28% of NFL players overall, including a stunning 67% of offensive linemen, had used steroids within the previous twelve months.

One 1973 survey found that 68% of participants in the 1972 Olympics reported steroid use—61% within six months of the event, partially prompting steroid testing at the next Olympics in 1976. The impact of Olympic performance enhancers is widespread and profound, symbolized by the first athlete to fail Olympic drug regulations, a woman: Panuta Rosani, a Polish discus thrower at the 1976 games. Two other athletes disqualifed but later reinstated, Ilona Slupianek (GDR) and Nadyezda Tkachenko (URS), returned to win titles in 1980. Any improper steroid use is arguably a sports blunder, although most abuse does little to influence world sports. The symbolic, if not real, effect of these first test failures caused sweeping changes in the world of sports, triggering drug tests by the NFL (1982) and later all pro sports plus the NCAA. The fate of these first athletes was to some degree inevitable—had they not been the first to be caught, others would have—hence the magnitude of their blunder should be tempered. Nonetheless, little has occurred in the sports world during the latter half of the twentieth century to rival the tidal wave of drug abuse and major sports testing.

Napoleon Lajoie

Who? Nap was a tenacious ball player on *and* off the field, becoming the first second baseman ever to be elected into the Hall of Fame. He played for 21 years, leading the American League in hitting four years in a row from

1901 through 1904 with some rather hefty averages of .422, .376, .355 and .381. (The peculiar spelling of his name presented problems with pronunciation from the start, with even his contemporaries having trouble. It was properly pronounced something like *LaZhwá* with a French twang—but few got it right, preferring to call him "Nap" instead.)

Knocking around a semi-pro league at age 20 in 1895, Nap was first discovered by the Fall River team in the New England minor league where he played 80 games. He promptly put up some big time numbers, batting .429 to lead the league including 163 hits and 94 runs scored. Mr. Lajoie had another peculiar trait: he attracted sports blunders like a magnet. The first was committed by the Boston National League franchise in 1895 when their scouts passed him up, citing he did not appear to be a good hitter. If the .429 average didn't impress them, one might have expected Nap's 34 doubles, 16 triples and 16 home runs might have—but they were unwavering in their expert assessment of his mediocrity. (Sounds familiar—perhaps the scouting profession has not improved much in the last 100 years or so.) The Philadelphia Phillies picked him up soon after along with another player from Fall River.

Joining the Phillies in mid-season, Nap played in just 39 games, distinguishing himself once again as he batted .327 in the big leagues with 57 hits. The following year was his first full big league season, and Nap was up to the task with a stunning .363 average, demonstrating a remarkable accuity for hitting doubles, leading the league with 40 in 1898 and topping the league again four more times in his career. At his retirement he had 650 total doubles, a record at the time and still a formidable number, considering career doubles by Pete Rose (746), Stan Musial (725), Honus Wagner (651), Hank Aaron(600), Rogers Hornsby (532) and Willie Mays (523), for example.

In 1899 and 1900, Nap continued his torrid hitting with averages of .380 and .346. By 1901, the new American League was launched and legendary baseball tycoon Connie Mack induced the youthful superstar to jump ship to his upstart Philadelphia Athletics team. Nap had plenty of incentive: his salary would go from the $2400 per year National League salary cap (no, salary caps are not a new thing) to $6000 in the American—plus Mack would give him a four year deal. But the move would not come easy. Lajoie was sued by his old team seeking an injunction under Baseball's forerunner to the reserve clause which mandated that players stick within their own league. It would have been easier, and probably more productive, had the Phillies and the National League increased or waived the salary cap, inducing Lajoie to stay put. Instead, they started a war, the second monster blunder to follow Nap's career. The court refused to enjoin Lajoie from switching, citing legal principles against "involuntary servitude." Nap would later lose on appeal but, for some obscure reason possibly rooted in revenge or maybe just stupidity, the Phillies did not retain their prize (the third Lajoie blunder) and effectively allowed the American League team to trade Lajoie to the American League Cleveland franchise where the Ohio courts refused to enjoin him from playing. By this time Nap had missed much of the 1902 season and failed to win the batting title that year. He was back in form for 1903 and 1904, though, winning titles at Cleveland with averages of .355 and .381. With a stellar career in Cleveland as a manager and player, Lajoie's charisma led to a new team nickname: the Cleveland Naps.

Historians credit Lajoie with launching the new American League, bringing instant credibility, charisma and success to the new league — probably much the same way Joe Namath aided the new American Football League in the 1960's. Soon after Lajoie's court battles, the National and American Leagues came to an accord in what would be the new "major league agreement" launching baseball's Major Leagues that we know today, at least indirectly due to the tenacious on and off-field performances by Lajoie.

CHAPTER THREE:
Boxed into a Corner

The next group of ten features a potpourri of bungles in football, baseball and tennis, but the group leads off with three straight boxing blunders that shaped the American sports scene. It also features the first of five episodes that are influenced by Muhammad Ali, who not only was one of the greatest athletes of all time, but who became one of the most visible and influential athletic figures in world history.

80 Sonny Liston

Sonny Liston made a mistake. Twice. It was Muhammad Ali, then known as Cassius Clay. Liston was a rough, mean heavyweight champion with relentless power. His fiery punch kindled fear in opponents' eyes the same evil way Mike Tyson would do three decades later. A veritable enforcer, Liston began knocking opponents around the ring in 1953, developing a ravenous appetite for one round knockouts.

On September 25, 1962, Liston challenged heavyweight champ Floyd Patterson in Chicago. The proud, gentlemanly Patterson took the fight straight to Liston and was rewarded with a devastating knockout of himself. When Patterson came to, both the fight crowd and his championship were gone. So was his future, for in his rematch Patterson was beaten before he started, evidenced by the pummeling he took before Liston dropped him in one round.

Meanwhile a noisy, mouthy Olympic light heavy from Louisville was as-
cending the pro heavyweight ranks, systematically clawing past two fighters
in 1960, eight in 1961 and six more in 1962 including an aging Archie Moore
who was TKO'd in the fourth round. In 1963 the ambitious Cassius Clay put
away three more progressively tougher opponents: Charlie Powell, Doug Jones
and Henry Cooper. Cooper was a savvy European fighter with a remarkably
high, somewhat protruding forehead that was a lightning rod for wicked
punches that normally split Cooper's skin during the course of a fight rendering him a bloody mess even in victory. Although the speedy Clay had cut
Cooper open and had him on the ropes literally as well as figuratively, Cooper
caught Clay napping with a thunderous left hook, dropping him to the canvas
like a listless sack of potatoes. According to Ali biographer Ferdie Pacheco,
who was Ali's fight doctor for much of his boxing career, Ali was saved only by
the bell and would have been too dazed to continue had his handler Angelo
Dundee not astutely found a tear in Clay's glove which caused a delay in the
action. When the fight continued in round five, a rejuvenated Cassius Clay
beat the vulnerable Cooper into a bloody mess, causing a stoppage of the fight
to save the defeated Cooper from bleeding to death.

The Cooper fight set the stage for Liston as Clay's next opponent. But
Liston took Clay lightly, barely even noticing until goaded into action by a
taunting campaign launched by the cunning, calculating Cassius Clay. He
coveted the championship bout, and Ali pulled out all the stops to force a
Liston confrontation. One day the massive Liston, nicknamed "the Bear"
for his bulk and power, actually found a bear trap in his yard planted by the
impish Clay who would go to any length to rile the champion. Eventually
the campaign worked, as Liston finally signed to fight Clay on February 1,
1964 in Miami Beach, Florida.

Fight pundits agreed: Liston the Bear was invulnerable, unbeatable.
The gamblers listed Clay as a 6-1 underdog, even laying odds on whether
Liston would actually kill Clay in the ring. But Clay was undaunted, waging
a war of words against a confused Liston that escalated right up to the day of
the fight weigh-in, including numerous drives by Liston's house where Clay

would stop, rant and rave at all hours of the day or night. Adding to the circus, Clay announced before the fight his conversion to the Muslim faith and unveiled his new name Muhammad Ali. At the weigh-in itself, Ali worked himself into a wild frenzy, citing poetry, chiding Liston and nearly bouncing off walls in a fit of pre-fight hysteria. Above it all, when confronted face to face by Ali, Liston had to look up at the surprisingly tall (6'3"), muscular Ali who looked down on the puzzled Liston in every sense of the word.

Whether confused, unimpressed, unprepared or maybe even over the hill, the invincible Liston entered the fight with no clue as to the speed, strength and resolve of a determined Muhammad Ali who had out-psyched Liston from day one. Even when Ali began the fight with dazzling speed, the experts were unimpressed and even felt vindicated when a charging Liston won the second round. But the next two rounds were vintage Ali who danced, moved and jabbed at the slower Liston with precision strikes, injuring Liston's shoulder and shredding his surprised face with rapid fire punishment.

In an ironic twist of fate that highlights the extent of Liston's blunders, even though it was ultimately a badly beaten Liston who could not emerge for the seventh round, it was Ali who nearly could not continue after round four. At the end of the fourth, Ali could not see either due to a foreign substance in his eye or maybe from a strike by Liston and he actually tried to quit until Angelo Dundee talked him out of it, chiding Ali to dance and avoid the killer Liston until his vision could clear up. That Ali did, and when the monolithic Liston caught on he nearly destroyed himself trying to level the quicker Ali. Eventually it was Liston with nothing left, and so he relinquished his title and refused to re-enter the ring for the next round. Through it all, had Liston been able to endure, or had he tagged his opponent when the elusive Ali could not see, perhaps history would have been different. But it was not to be. Ali had held on, and the championship was his.

Ali would not fight again for exactly fifteen months until his rematch with Liston on May 25, 1965, in Lewistown, Maine. This time a supposedly wiser, still powerful, but slower and mentally defeated Liston would crumble in one round, succumbing to a cross-over right hand to the head. Liston was dropped to the floor but not out cold as Ali hovered and taunted the stunned Liston who eventually rose again ready to fight, taking several extra seconds to get up as Ali was escorted to a neutral corner by referee Jersey Joe Walcott who would return to call the fight over by a knockout.

Liston would later publicly explain why he was slow to rise, suggesting he was afraid of the crazy Ali who he feared would smash him down if he attempted to right himself. The Ali psych-job, of course, had worked to perfection. In the words of Dr. Ferdie Pacheco, Liston had actually lost both championship fights at the first fight weigh-in. So he did—and the rest is history.

79 Mike Tyson

He was the second coming of Sonny Liston. The kid Mike Tyson from Brooklyn, one of the fiercest punchers in boxing history, won his first 19 professional fights in a row by knockout. On November 22, 1986, at the age of just twenty years, Tyson won the WBC heavyweight crown by a second round knockout of Trevor Berbick. He then knocked off the WBA and IBF champions to gain the undisputed title in 1987. In 1988 Tyson scored an impressive fourth round TKO of Larry Holmes, followed by a knockout of Michael Spinks in the first round and proving himself as a one-man wrecking crew with youth, quickness and unbridled power.

In 1989 Tyson had to battle the challenging spoils of victory as personal problems mounted, including a bitter divorce from his actress wife Robin Givens. By February 10, 1990, Tyson's problems caught up as he was knocked out by then unknown James "Buster" Douglas in Japan. Douglas immediately lost his newly acquired title to Evander Holyfield, and Mike Tyson scheduled a Holyfield bout in hopes of regaining his heavyweight title in November of 1991. As fate would have it, Tyson injured a rib in training and had to postpone the match, and in the interim, Tyson was charged and tried for raping a Black Miss America contestant in Indianapolis. In February of 1992 he was found guilty, receiving a six year sentence.

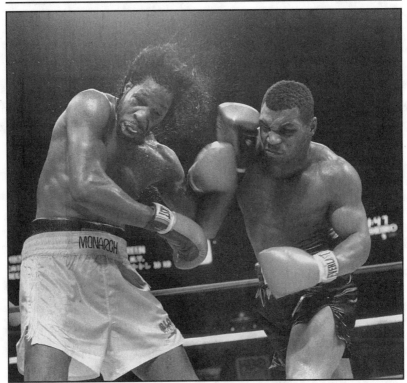

A youthful Mike Tyson defeated all opponents — except himself. (Photo by Rick Harbus UPI/Corbis-Bettmann)

By 1995 Tyson was back in the ring, disposing of stiff Peter McNeeley in just 89 seconds and landing a $25 million paycheck for the trouble. Combined with prior signing bonuses of $15 million from Showtime and the MGM Grand, Tyson raked in $40 million total for 1996 according to the annual *Forbes* Magazine roundup. This left Tyson in the number two spot for highest paid athletes, one notch behind Michael Jordan's $43.9 million. The following year Tyson did even better, knocking Michael off the top spot with $75 million to MJ's $52.6 million, making Tyson the highest paid athlete in the history of sports.

Had Tyson not self-destructed with personal problems contributing to a needless loss, followed by his senseless rendezvous with fate that led to a rape conviction, there is no telling what Tyson could have accomplished. With his youthful energy, power and confidence Mike Tyson may have rivaled the great Ali in boxing accomplishment, and he certainly would have

49

set earnings records of staggering proportions. As it is, he did remarkably well, even though his three year forced layoff interrupted destiny—until he blundered yet again in biting off a chunk of Evander Holyfield's ear in a 1997 match. A lifetime suspension ensued, although Tyson's career was largely over anyway.

The Dempsey-Tunney Long Count

There are those who might argue the fabled long count, a blunder to be sure, should not receive a significant ranking, but the scope of the long count misadventure coupled with the sheer enormity of the championship event in the context of the times renders it worthy of historical merit.

The grandeur of the Jack Dempsey-John Tunney confrontation was of gladiator proportions, a magnitude comparable to—maybe even exceeding—modern day Superbowls. Heavyweight prize fighting was at a zenith during the 1920's, boxing's golden era that never would be matched, although it would undergo a significant historical resurgence during the Ali years from 1960 to 1980. Five times between 1921 and 1927 title bout gate receipts would exceed $1 million each, milestones that would not be seen for more than two generations—an especially amazing feat when adjusted for inflation. Remarkably, the heavyweight legend "Manassa Mauler" Jack Dempsey would participate in all five such fights. One was the famous 1927 long count fight before 105,000 feverish fans at Chicago's historic Soldier Field. The era was dominated by boxing's precursor to promoter Don King: one Tex Rickard, who promoted all five of Dempsey's monster fight gates, including the Dempsey-Tunney rematch.

Jack Dempsey was a tenacious champion, a street fighting mauler who would sink his teeth into an opponent and never let go. Not large by today's heavyweight standards, Dempsey, who hovered around 190 pounds, was more than big and tough enough for his era. His chief nemesis grew to be Gene Tunney, less of a brawler and more of a boxer, who defeated Dempsey in their first championship fight in 1926. The rematch would be a year later in September of 1927, and the build-up reflected one of the most antici-pated events in sports history.

As fight day approached Chicago's hotels bulged from hoards of fans, reporters and gamblers. About 14,000 downtown Chicago hotel rooms were booked in advance, and the New York Central and Michigan Central rail-roads expected 22,000 people to wedge their way onto Chicago bound trains. Gambling insiders expected to see $10,000,000 waged on the fight, with twenty percent of that coming from New York alone, and the odds makers favored Tunney slightly at 7 to 5.

Meanwhile the Chicago Police Department canceled vacations and as-signed 2,800 uniformed officers and detectives to Soldier Field which itself already had arranged over 2,000 ushers, 400 ticket takers, 400 more ticket inspectors, plus a 150 man fire brigade. On the night of the fight 104,943 official spectators jammed into the stadium, inspiring these poetic remarks from one unnamed reporter:

"The veil of darkness over it all; the rippling sea of humanity stretching out as far as the eye could see; the Doric columns of Soldier Field glow-ing a soft white along the upper battlements of the arena; and finally the ring itself where two men would fight it out with their fists in a pool of white light—these were the high spots of an unforgettable spectacle."

Gate receipts would be a stunning $2,658,660 with $990,000 pledged to Tunney (who reportedly wrote his own check for $10,000 to the promoter for the difference so he could hold a $1 million check in the end) with about half of that going to Dempsey—at the time the largest purse ever allocated to a non-champion.

As the match wore on, it appeared Tunney the boxer was forging ahead on points. About a minute into the seventh round Dempsey landed a cross-over right hand to Tunney's head, followed by two more punches finding their mark before a rapid fire fourth punch, a wicked left hook, caught Tunney as he rebounded off the ropes, leveling the champion. After the fight Dempsey would admit he had hit Tunney with every punch he dreamed of during the past year. Tunney was out could, but then the blunder. Dempsey the street fighter had a habit of hovering over his downed opponents so he could smash them again as they tried to get up. But the rules had changed. Now the standing fighter was required to retreat to a neutral corner; Dempsey, though, hovered at a non-neutral corner near the downed Tunney, a little further than he used to when he was ready to sucker punch fighters if they dared to stand, but the fight referee was still not satisfied. The ref grabbed Dempsey and shoved him across the ring to the neutral site, and by the time he returned the referee began counting at "one," interrupting the official knockdown time keeper who was already at "five" and causing the count to start over. The crowd of 105,000 was going wild; reporters instinctively began to sniff for a "fix." Tunney came to, but stayed on one knee until the nine-count to take advantage of the respite, buying himself about 15 to 17 total seconds. Still wobbly, Tunney rose and searched for answers. He wasn't ready to attack yet, and he feared going into a clutch with Dempsey who would surely land an upper cut rabbit punch, possibly finishing him off, so Tunney elected to err on the "valor" side of discretion: he retreated, circling the ring backwards and ducking at least eight Dempsey punches.

As Tunney's head cleared he abandoned the backpedaling in favor of attack. After a brief flurry of punches, Tunney landed a straight right to the jaw, and later demolished Dempsey with a stunning shot to the chest. Dempsey did not go down, but everyone knew the end was approaching. In the eighth round Dempsey did hit the canvas, but only for a short count, and Dempsey kept fighting to the bitter end. Both fighters were still standing at the final bell, in fact they kept slugging until their corner men pulled them apart.

Tunney was the victor, ending the great Jack Dempsey era once and for all. Whether Gene Tunney could have recovered from a normal count after he crumbled to the floor is sheer speculation, but he certainly benefited from the extra seconds to clear himself to continue. Dempsey's failure to immediately seek a neutral corner may have cost him the title and probably changed the course of boxing history as the fabled "long count" became a permanent part of American sports lore.

Ted Turner vs. Bowie Kuhn

As long standing commissioner of Major League Baseball for fifteen tumultuous years from 1969 to 1984, Bowie Kuhn was one of the most sued men in America. At the end of his first year, Kuhn denied Curt Flood his free agency leading to Flood's famous, but losing antitrust case. Kuhn oversaw the Andy Messersmith case which led directly to player free agency (see the "Messersmith" section, #10); investigated Cubs manager Leo Durocher; feuded with Oakland owner Charlie Finley; suspended Yankees owner George Steinbrenner; lost every significant battle with player union chief Marvin Miller; and was rocked back on his heels in and out of court by the forceful Braves owner and mega-entrepreneur Ted Turner.

· In 1976 Major League Baseball and the players' association negotiated a new collective bargaining agreement with a complex series of free agency terms. In conjunction with the free agency rules, Commissioner Kuhn invoked a number of anti-tampering directives to prevent premature negotiations with forthcoming free agents. In September of 1976 Kuhn fined the Atlanta Braves for tampering with the Giants' home run slugger Gary Matthews, revoking the Braves' first round pick in the forthcoming baseball draft.

A month later during an impromptu cocktail party at the New York Yankee hospitality suite in the Waldorf Towers, Braves owner Ted Turner cornered Bob Lurie, owner of the San Francisco Giants, and in front of various reporters brought up the subject of Matthews, the league leading home run hitter for the past three seasons. Lurie begged off, suggesting league rules prevented Turner's intrusion until November 4. Apparently that revved Turner up, who responded by inviting Lurie to a Gary Matthews welcome party in Atlanta, a high profile affair complete with its own signboard at the airport, "Welcome to Atlanta, Gary Matthews."

These and other Turner comments made great copy for the media, and Kuhn, who disliked the roguish Turner anyway, was livid. Turner himself warmed up to the confrontation, later informing staffers that Kuhn would probably suspend him since a fine would do no good and Kuhn would be reluctant to punish Matthews by preventing him from signing with Turner's Braves.

Several weeks later Turner was observed outside the Los Angeles Hilton screaming to the surprised world, "Bowie Kuhn is going to kill me...my life is over!" When L.A. reporters got wind of Turner's antics, he told the L.A. Times that "Kuhn's going to gun me down in this hotel like a dog!"

Turner got his wish, of sorts, for Commissioner Kuhn suspended the Braves owner for a year, during which Turner was delighted to go sailing. Turner also sued Kuhn in federal court in Georgia contesting the commissioner's powers to act unilaterally against Turner and the Braves. League commissioners are, for legal purposes, heads of private associations. As such, they are not governed by Constitutional due process requirements which are founded upon governmental "state" action, but they still must adhere to certain minimal standards of private sector due process referred to in the legal community as "fundamental fairness." The first requirement is for a commissioner not to stray from his own league rules in handling an internal controversy. In Turner's case the appropriate written constraints were to be found in the Major League Agreement, the related bylaws of Major League Baseball, and the collective bargaining agreement in place at the time. Absent a provision to the contrary, Kuhn was not prevented from exercising his "best interests of baseball" powers to suspend Turner, but as it happens he did violate a specific provision when he usurped a Braves draft choice. Whether Kuhn could have prevented Matthews from signing with the Braves at all is debatable, but the commissioner voluntarily refrained from blocking Matthews, presumably because he desired to avoid an anti-player posture. This may have been a blunder on Kuhn's part, one of several that contributed to the Kuhn-Turner ordeal.

First, Turner turned the whole affair into a public relations masterpiece with everyone from the governor of Georgia to the Atlanta mayor turning against Kuhn. Published sources also report thousands of complaint letters flooding the general offices of Major League Baseball, and Turner is credited with infiltrating the league offices by obtaining a list of all the complainers which became the foundation for a season ticket sale campaign. Second, Turner got to take a year off on his boat. Third, Turner won part of the legal battle by overturning the Braves' lost first round draft pick. And finally, after all the legal dust settled, Gary Matthews became a Brave anyway, giving all ballplayers a taste of what free agency was all about. Ted Turner didn't just win, he made a fool of the egotistical Kuhn with his antics and victories—on and off the field.

Denny McLain

In 1934 Dizzy Dean, an amiable pitcher with a sweet country drawl, was a 30-game winner in the major leagues. No pitcher would do so again until Denny McLain's masterpiece year of 1968 when he went 31-6 for Detroit as the Tigers won the World Series for the first time since 1945.

McLain was a moderate goat just the year before, winning 17 games but missing his last six starts due to a peculiar—and somewhat doubted—injury to his toe. The Tigers narrowly missed the Series that year, and McLain took some of the blame for his inability to perform. He had already established himself as a noteworthy pitcher since he was brought up in 1963, winning 16 games in 1965 and 20 more in 1966.

In 1968, after "helping" Detroit blow it in 1967, fans booed McLain at the beginning of the season but fan discontent failed to last long as he began to accumulate victories. By mid-July he was already 18-2, a career year for most pitchers. On the first of September monster hitter Boog Powell smashed a line drive that McLain converted into a triple play to hold onto victory number 27. In one of his more poignant moments, McLain faced aging icon Mickey Mantle during Mantle's last game in Tiger Stadium late in 1968. Leading 6-1 in what would be McLain's victory number 31, his last of the season, McLain grooved a pitch down the pipe for Mickey who promptly cracked a homer bumping him past Jimmie Foxx on the all-time list, the next to the last home run of Mantle's entire career. McLain finished the season with an eye-popping earned run average of 1.96 and 28 complete games, winning the Cy Young Award. He struggled in the World Series against the St. Louis Cardinals, but he did win game six on two days rest allowing Tiger Mickey Lolich to beat a tough Bob Gibson in game seven for the championship.

Denny McLain took to the ensuing fame and show biz like a parched duck to Walden's Pond, but perhaps that was his downfall or, at least, the beginning of the end. Becoming cocky and brash, McLain showed up on the Ed Sullivan TV show and in a Las Vegas lounge act. Meanwhile the Tigers awarded a then lofty $100,000-a-year contract, and he won the Cy Young a second time in 1969 with a record of 24-9 and a Tigers record nine shutouts. During 1969 McLain showed hints of self destructive tendencies, blowing off his all-star game start and failing to show up until the fourth inning.

By the following year the wheels came off, Commissioner Bowie Kuhn suspending McLain three months for bookmaking offenses. He filed for bankruptcy, got suspended again, and later was traded to the Washington Senators where he lost 22 games in 1971. At age 28 it was all over as Denny McLain, an overweight "has been," struggled and failed at numerous businesses. He almost could be a sympathetic figure now in his twilight, but in May of 1997 he was sentenced to eight years in prison for stealing a reported $2.5 million from his company's pension fund, which itself went bankrupt 18 months after McLain bought it. He was also ordered to repay the entire amount as restitution, and according to his lawyer McLain expected to lose everything but his house.

McLain's blunders get high marks for feeblemindedness, plus they likely did much to shape the sports record books. In his middle twenties Denny McLain was a dominant pitcher, the likes of which had not been seen for thirty-four years, and his record performances have not been matched since. He had won a staggering 55 games in two seasons, 92 games over a four year span. But fame, arrogance, and temptation caught up with McLain as he did a "crash and burn" act that continues into the late 1990's.

Charlie Finley's Managers

Colorful Athletics owner Charlie Finley was, on balance, good for baseball. He brought irreverence to a sport that periodically goes into a funk, once selling three of his star players outright, angering the egotistical and powerful commissioner Bowie Kuhn who vetoed the sale as being "against the best interests of baseball." In 1976 Finley sued Kuhn in federal court in Chicago (Finley was a Chicagoan) to overturn Kuhn's edict, hoping to complete his sale of Joe Rudi and Rollie Fingers to the Red Sox (for $2 million) and Vida Blue to the Yankees ($1.5 million). Even though Kuhn's intervention might qualify for some type of blunder in its own right (years before, Babe Ruth was sold from the Red Sox to the Yankees, and legendary owner Connie Mack was notorious for dumping his players) Finley lost his case, the court upholding Kuhn's broad powers to monitor, among other things, the "competitive balance" of the league.

This and other misdeeds led Finley to christen Kuhn the "village idiot," whereupon Finley thought it over and apologized for insulting village idiots everywhere. But Kuhn and others may have considered returning the compliment for some of Charlie's own antics, one of which continued a pattern of bizarre conduct for 13 straight years. At least one publication referred to the 1959 to 1971 A's era as Finley's "reign of terror" when he scrubbed A's managers thirteen straight times. From 1959 to 1969 the A's finished as high as 6th place only once, normally languishing between 7th and 9th in the standings. Then in 1969 the A's shot up to second under their 11th manager Hank Bauer. Even so, Finley was on a roll, firing Bauer in September of their second place season and replacing him with John McNamara who guided the team to second place again in 1970. By then Finley finally found Dick Williams as the lucky 13th manager, and he finally engineered a pennant for Charlie's Oakland A's. Williams soon quit, but at least he become the first of Finley's managers to last a minimum of two seasons.

Although Finley's deeds and misdeeds score high stupidity marks, their cumulative effect on baseball in total are debatable. Nonetheless, his mischievous changes probably helped mire the A's near the bottom of the standings for a decade, then for whatever reason his fortuitous find in Dick Williams likely propelled the A's to one of the great modern day championship reins in the early 1970's. Charlie's antics are probably best recognized in the totality, symbolically ushering in the new gunslinging, irreverent breed of baseball owners such as Ted Turner, George Steinbrenner and Finley himself. These new hipshooters changed the face of American baseball, giving it a shot in the arm during the 1970's and 1980's before crumbling with a loss of fans and ratings in the nineties.

One footnote: Charlie did at least one more thing. He hired a runner in his Chicago office who had an extraordinary resemblance to the youthful, cherub-like countenance of baseball slugger Hammerin' Hank Aaron, so the other office workers appropriately dubbed him "Hammer." The name stuck, as most folks would later recognize him as M.C. Hammer.

The Super Bowl Patriots

Although the New England Patriots of 1985-86 lost Super Bowl XX in spectacular fashion, setting a record in futility by losing to the Chicago Bears by the widest margin ever at that time, one really can't blame poor performance alone as a blunder. But just after their Super Bowl loss, the Boston Globe reported drug use by six of the Patriot players. Whether these drugs were supposed to enhance performance or not, clearly team play was not of a caliber equal to a monster Bears team of all-pros such as Dan Hampton, Walter Payton, Mike Singletary, Richard Dent and Jim McMahon, not to mention "Refrigerator" Perry and names like Wilson, Marshall, Hilgenberg, Galt, McKinnon and others.

The public backlash stemming from the Globe stories caused NFL commissioner Pete Rozelle and others to implement a formal drug testing program. When the head of the NFL Players Association, Gene Upshaw, objected strongly to any sort of random testing, the NFL charged ahead to implement a hasty drug program, itself becoming a serious sports blunder noted immediately below.

Richard Dent vs. The NFL Drug Policy

In his haste to curb legitimate concerns about a mounting drug problem in the NFL, Pete Rozelle pressed his powers as commissioner to the limit, implementing his own random testing program over the objections of NFLPA chief Gene Upshaw. On the heels of the Glove article on Patriots players drug use, this led directly to a formal arbitration where the players union contested Rozelle's actions.

Rozelle and the NFL argued that the commissioner's "integrity of the game" powers were well settled historically and remained unchanged by the most recent 1982 collective bargaining negotiations. The arbitrator considered the impact of collective bargaining upon Rozelle's authority, the confidentiality issues of random testing, and the legitimate interests of the league in controlling drug abuse. In so doing the arbitrator gleaned enough language from the collective bargaining agreement to support Rozelle's powers in general, but to strike down his specific ability to implement random "spot" testing.

Shortly thereafter, this author had personal occasion to dissect the NFL drug policy thoroughly in representing Chicago Bear and Superbowl MVP Richard Dent in a court action against the NFL and its drug policy in 1988. At the time the drug policy was a mishmash without firm definitions or procedural safeguards.

Dent successfully challenged his suspension and certain specific elements of the drug policy in Cook County Circuit Court in Chicago. In so doing Dent became the first NFL player to challenge and change the drug policy in court. It all started when Dent was asked to take a random drug test on August 23, 1988, on one day's notice. Dent refused, citing several tests he had taken during the prior year, criticizing the NFL notice and hearing provisions of the drug testing process. The policy at that time was a source of great confusion, as the 1982 collective bargaining agreement provided for periodic testing on a pre-scheduled basis, such as in training camp. If a player tested positive for any of the prohibited substances, which included minimum alcohol levels, cocaine and marijuana (plus the usual steroid performance enhancers), then the player was placed on a reasonable cause list. The term "reasonable cause" was a euphemism for "random testing," and was therefore suspect from the get-go. If a player tested positive from a scheduled test, he was placed on the reasonable cause list. If he were to test positive again, then he was subject to an automatic four game suspension. A third test would find the player suspended for life, although he could attempt to reapply after one year.

At the time of Dent's suspension he was already on a reasonable cause list stemming from a prior test a year earlier that allegedly was positive for traces of marijuana. But Dent and other players at the time were never informed when the reasonable cause period would terminate and, more importantly, the players were never informed formally of any test result. During its infancy, the NFL drug program did not utilize written notice to the players, instead giving oral notice to team trainers who, in turn, would tell the appropriate player—if they remembered, or chose, to do so. When Dent challenged his suspension his legal counsel (yours truly) discovered that certain terms of the NFL drug policy ran exactly contrary to the NFL bylaws governing the league as a whole. The drug rules provided a player could be automatically suspended for a second positive test or for refusing to take a test. However, the governing bylaws stated that a person couldn't be suspended without a hearing. Because of this inconsistency Dent, who was suspended with no prior hearing, was able to state a claim in court which resulted in a lightning fast settlement. Richard came to us on a Wednesday, Thursday the case was filed, and on Friday it was settled in the judge's chambers. (Then on Sunday the Bears beat the Colts and Richard had an especially good game, so the author unabashedly accepts partial credit for the win—one of only a few football victories partially engineered by a word processor.)

There were two basic outgrowths of the Dent case in the National Football League. First, players get written notice of drug test results. Second, it has been clarified that players have an opportunity for a hearing in conjunction with a suspension. The notice provisions are especially significant, because under the old rules it was possible for a player to be suspended for a second violation without even knowing about the first one. What if the first test result was a mistake? And if it wasn't, then much time would lapse before getting much needed help to the player. Either way the lack of notice was a dangerous flaw, and written notice was a specific outgrowth of the Dent case.

The original NFL drug policy, though well intentioned, ran afoul of collective bargaining agreement due to the random testing features, and thereafter continued to run contrary to the NFL bylaws. The original policy also had confidentiality problems, for any system of oral notices running through the trainer's office is begging for information leaks anywhere from the lab to the locker room. Today confidentiality is mandated, with heavy fines for any individual or team breaching the appropriate channels of information flow.

Drugs have regrettably become a major influence upon sports and individual athletes. The pre-Dent NFL drug policy may have caused more problems than it solved, though no one will ever really know its true deficiencies, but it was a needless blunder at its inception.

Monica Seles

Tennis dynamo Monica Seles was born on December 2, 1973 in Yugoslavia. Just under fourteen years later she was on the pro tennis circuit, and by 1990 Seles was the French Open champion. A year later she topped Steffi Graf as the number one woman player in the world en route to winning seven of the next nine grand slam events.

In April of 1993, when Seles was at the top of her game and still not yet 20 years old, during a match she was stabbed in the back with a nine inch knife by a demented fan attempting to propel Graf back to the number one

Only a deranged tennis fan could halt the Seles juggernaut.
(Photo by Bruno Torres, UPI/Corbis-Bettmann)

ranking. The injury was not nearly so severe as could have been expected, so most tennis pundits expected Monica to miss only about four weeks. Instead she missed the rest of the year and was slow to reenter the game with reports of severe (and highly understandable) psychological damage to the teenage phenomenon. Seles did return successfully, but has never quite mastered the dominance she displayed at her peak, depriving the tennis world of its young superstar on the rise.

Although the stabbing certainly changed the landscape of contemporary tennis, the game will survive the incident. Seles herself was hit hard, however, not only psychologically but in her pocketbook as well. In 1995 Stefi Graf was the only woman on the *Forbes Magazine* list of the top forty compensated athletes, footnoted with this reference to Seles: "The only woman [Graf] on this year's Super 40, but count on Monica Seles to return in 1996."

Seles did not return to the list.

If rated by stupidity alone, the selfishly cruel, reprehensible actions of her attacker would rank in the blunder list top ten. Stabbing a teenage tennis player in the back during a match tops the Tonya Harding fiasco and is certainly more abhorrent than Pete Rose gambling or the Red Sox losing Carlton Fisk, for example, but fortunately Seles was not seriously injured and did return to the pro tour. Although less disgusting, the actions of the Red Sox in dumping Babe Ruth or the 1963 enlargement of the strike zone had greater long term relative impact on the sport of baseball, but the Seles episode is worthy of due contempt and reflection as one of top 100 bad moves in sports.

George Blanda Goes West

In radically different ways both pro football and the author matured in the late 1960's and early 70's. Occasionally our paths would cross, as when the feisty, rough and tumble Oakland Raiders of the old AFL would perform their act on television during the days of their up and coming young quarterbacks Daryle Lamonica and Kenny "Snake" Stabler.

During those years the Raiders sported one of the most colorful, tenacious and *oldest* pro football players in memory, George Blanda. Both a place kicker and quarterback, George was a rising star for the Bears from his first year in 1949 until he lost his starting QB job due to an injury. Even so, he was a Bear mainstay until time appeared to catch up and he was released in 1959 at age 31, then a ten year NFL veteran. Teams developed a habit of underestimating Blanda's longevity, prematurely cutting him due to age, the Oilers were next, dumping Blanda *eight* years later at the ripe old age of 39, well beyond the life span of nearly all NFL players. But Blanda caught on with the Oakland Raiders, performing place kicker magic and filling in at back-up quarterback.

As a Raider, the seasoned pro Blanda displayed a penchant for coming off the bench to rescue young buck quarterback Daryle Lamonica at the end of several games, amazing Raiders head coach John Madden, himself nine years younger than Blanda. *Twelve years* after the Bears released him, Blanda was still going strong. At age 43 Blanda was brought in to call signals against the Steelers before half-time, throwing two touchdown passes and kicking a field goal to help engineer a 31-14 Raiders victory. A week later Blanda trotted out in the closing seconds of the annual Raiders-Chiefs brawl with Oakland trailing by three. He responded by coolly kicking a 48-yard field goal to earn a tie game at 17 all.

The very next week a war was scheduled to take place between the Raiders and their hated rivals, the Cleveland Browns. Blanda had never beaten Cleveland in all his playing years, so the ageless warrior was particularly focused. Early in the first quarter Blanda kicked a 43-yarder for three points and a Raiders lead, adding another in the second quarter after a Lamonica touchdown pass for a 13-0 Raiders advantage. The Browns came back before half-time, cutting their deficit to 13-10. In the third period the Raiders drove to the Browns 19 yard line but failed to score, with even Blanda missing a short field goal attempt. A long Cleveland run propelled the Browns over Oakland at 17-13, and with just over ten minutes to play in the game Lamonica was dropped by defensive end Ron Snidow, severely injuring his left shoulder.

Coach Madden looked around the bench and spied Blanda, the ageless wonder. Blanda couldn't move the team, so the Raiders punted away, only to find the Browns kicking another field goal to extend their lead to 20-13. To make matters worse, Blanda was intercepted on the next series, so when Oakland got the ball again with 4:11 to play the venerable George Blanda became a gladiator possessed. Picking apart the Browns' defense, Blanda willed the Raiders down to the Cleveland 31, only to stall there at fourth and 16 yards to go. Tension mounted and sweat cascaded off the weary temples of players and coaches as the unflappable Blanda threw an awkward strike to the human glue stick Fred Biletnikoff for a first down. Blanda was hit hard on the play, and the Raiders called time out. Blanda argued for a pass play and the beleaguered Madden relented. Blanda gunned a pass to receiver Warren Wells in the end zone, Blanda kicked the extra point and suddenly the score was tied at 20 with 79 seconds remaining on the game clock.

Cleveland proceeded to milk the clock and move the ball into position for the winning field goal when Raiders corner Kent McCloughan wrestled a pass from a Browns receiver for the interception. Blanda climbed from his seat on the bench, gulped for oxygen, strapped on his battered helmet and trotted onto the field. His first pass was incomplete, and then he was tackled for a 10 yard loss. With just 16 seconds left and no time outs, Blanda threw incomplete. The Raiders gained four yards on third down but were called for a penalty. Had the Browns accepted the penalty, the Raiders would have faced fourth down and a possible 56-yard field goal, an NFL record tying distance at the time (although Saints kicker Tom Dempsey would ironically set a new record of 63 yards that very day), a formidable feat for a 43-year-old kicker. Remarkably, Cleveland accepted the penalty, presumably to back Blanda up even further, giving the Raiders one more shot at third down.

Blanda responded by completing a nine yard out pattern, stopping the clock at seven seconds on the 45 yard line setting up a 52 yard field goal possibility. With Lamonica injured, the Raiders were left with Ken Stabler to hold, but it failed to faze the unflappable Blanda who launched the 52-yarder through the goal posts for the 251st field goal of his career and a spectacular, if not historic, Raiders win by three points: 23-20.

According to NFL records, Blanda was far from through. The following week he beat Denver 24-19 with a last minute touchdown pass, and the week after Blanda kicked a field goal at the gun to down the Chargers 20-17. All he did at age 43 was rescue five games in a row from defeat, after which he was officially named NFL player of the year for his superhuman efforts.

Even with all that, George Blanda played yet *another five years*, not hanging up the cleats until 1976 when he was 48 years old, a little long in the tooth but a dignified warrior nonetheless. Meanwhile, the Chicago Bears would occasionally have an adequate quarterback, such as their championship year in 1963, but they wouldn't land another legitimate star until Jim McMahon was drafted in 1982. The Raiders, on the other hand, carried Blanda for ten years after his career was over a second time, grooming and polishing Oakland's younger talents Daryle Lamonica and Kenny Stabler. Snake Stabler in particular became a superstar in his own right, wise and cagey beyond his years—a coincidence, or yet another Blanda-inspired chapter of NFL lore?

CHAPTER FOUR:
The 3 T's: Terrorism, Thuggery and Taunting

The countdown to 61 includes terrorism, violence, and taunting, three negative elements that have crept into sports over the years, accelerating since the 1970's. It would be tempting to include Jack Tatum's vile hit on football receiver Darryl Stingley, but the play in question was arguably a hard, even dirty hit, but nonetheless a part of football that could be defined as a "playing error" that fails to qualify for the blunder list. Is Tatum's thuggery worth mentioning, especially since he writes freely about his role as assassin? Absolutely, especially since it contributed to the "no spearing" rules in football, but the author has included Kermit Washington's demolition of Rudy Tomjonovich's face instead because it was a vicious punch intending precisely the harm delivered and was clearly not part of the game of basketball. It was a bad idea, pure and simple, a blunder in the truest sense.

Yankees Fire Stengel

There are few baseball legends as storied as Casey Stengel, who played for the Dodgers, Pirates, Phillies, Giants and Braves before attaining icon status as manager for the Dodgers, Braves, Yankees and Mets. Some historians would call him the greatest manager of all time, and they might not be wrong. Not only did he manage the Yankees to ten pennants and seven World Series victories during their dynasty years from 1949 to 1960, he

Once a Yankee always a Yankee? (UPI/Corbis-Bettman)

became the first manager for the newly christened Mets after the Yankees dumped him. Stengel also re-wrote baseball lingo with his wit, charm and earthy insights to the grand game of baseball.

Stengel, whose name was a tribute to his home town of Kansas City ("K.C."), performed as a capable player, a journeyman with character and flair. In 1916, for example, he hit .364 as a Brooklyn Dodger in the World Series. In 1919, while playing for the Pittsburgh Pirates against Brooklyn, Stengel stuffed a live bird under his cap, and when he came to bat he tipped his hat to the crowd causing the bird to fly out and the crowd went wild. Apparently the Pirates were unimpressed, for they traded him to Philadelphia before the season was over. Stengel would play in the World Series again, but by 1925 his career as a player came to a close. He became manager of the minor league Toledo Mud Hens in 1926, a post he held for about five years until the team went belly up. He was hired as a coach for the Dodgers in 1931, and almost immediately attained manager where he languished until the team fired him in 1936. By 1938 he was back, this time with the Boston Bees (later known as the Boston Braves) where he managed for six years without finishing higher than fifth place.

After bouncing around various leagues for five more years, including the Pacific Coast League, the general manager of the Yankees, a good friend of Casey's, summoned him to take over the pinstripers in 1949. His first press conference included a self-deprecating reference to barely knowing where he was at, causing the baseball press to dismiss him as some sort of clown. They were partly right, but he also turned out to be a darned good manager, taking the third place Yankees to a World Series championship his first year.

He followed that with four more in a row, breaking records for both consecutive pennants and World Series championships.

The team he took over sported many superstars, including Joe DiMaggio, but Stengel took a risk that few would dare, rebuilding the team around just three marquee players: Slugging speedster Mickey Mantle, catcher Yogi Berra and pitcher Whitey Ford. The rest of the team included roll players who were platooned and kept hungry to play (sounding, in principle at least, somewhat like the NBA Chicago Bulls and their roll players led by savvy coach Phil Jackson), performing at or above their talent levels at all times. Stengel was prone to other eccentricities, many of which were ahead of his time, such as utilizing some of his best pitchers as relievers.

Although the Yankee teams Stengel built and managed won relentlessly, even when they stumbled they did it in style. In 1954 the Yankees finished second, but they still won a staggering 103 games! And the next year they were back in first again, taking league pennants also in 1956, 1957 and 1958. New York was third in 1959 as the White Sox fielded their now famous go-go World Series team, but the pinstripers won the pennant again in 1960. Nonetheless, Stengel was fired—not only for failing to beat the Pirates in the 1960 Series but, remarkably, for simply being too old, prompting this Stengel commentary: "I'll never make the mistake of being seventy again." When a room full of sports writers asked Casey what he would do next, they got an earful of this Stengelism, "Have another drink!"

If the Stengel story ended there—and, of course, it does not—it would still be quite a blunder, for although the Yankees made some hay with Mantle and Maris in 1961, they never again achieved the unrivaled dominance of either the Ruth era or the Mantle years under the watchful, colorful guidance of one remarkable Casey Stengel. In twelve glorious seasons under Casey, the Bronx Bombers made more records than the Beatles: Most years managing an American League champion (10); most consecutive first place finishes (5); most World Series games managed (63); and most World Series wins (37). All told, in twelve years Stengel won the Series an astonishing seven times.

Adding to the lore of Stengel, the crusty Casey went from top to bottom, becoming the first manager of the hapless Mets in 1962. "It's great to be back in the Polar Grounds again with the New York knickerbockers," observed Stengel. Dryly.

The first decade of the Mets became one of the most storied in baseball history as the new National Leaguers finished a painfully dismal 40-120 in 1962, only to evolve into the "Miracle Mets" of 1969 as they—and a ton of pitching—won the World Series. Although Stengel wasn't around as manager beyond 1965, his did much to put the Mets on the map, once again proving winners had a peculiar habit of following Stengel. Meanwhile the 1965 Yankees were mired in the second division as the Stengel-built Mets continued to improve from jokes to journeymen to champions.

One footnote to Stengel's Mets: Marv Throneberry, klutz first baseman on the 1962 team, made the brilliant move of holding out for more money in the spring of 1963 following one of the worst team performances in history with 120 losses. The inimitable Marv, who himself hit a whopping .238 with 49 accidental RBI's and led the league in fielding errors, was promptly shipped off to the minor leagues in Buffalo.

"No Mas"

Marvelous Marvin Hagler. Tommy "Hit Man" Hearns. Sugar Ray Leonard. Roberto Duran.

There can be more than one golden era in a given sport, and in the 1970's and 1980's the lighter boxers, the middleweights and welterweights, were reborn to rival the big guys who were on their last legs after a great run during the sixties and much of the seventies. These smaller fighters were fast, strong and fierce—and great entertainers. Some stood out more than others; some were great boxers, others just great fighters. Duran was the latter. Roberto Duran would stare into the face of his opponent, his own cold, steely eyes reminiscent of the lifeless pupils of a killer shark, staring straight through his challenger, cruelly dismissing each fighter to defeat each new ego before relentlessly ripping through the fighter's unsuspecting defenses. In winning one of his titles from the well muscled, taller Iran Barkley, Duran stalked Barkely for much of the fight, finally taking a wicked shot to the head by Barkely in the latter rounds. Duran was rocked sideways and backward on his heels, but his knees refused to buckle. Duran shook off the blow in seconds, gathering his wits quickly before continuing his unrequited stalking of the champion Barkley. The ring announcers could not fathom Duran's staying power and, presumably, neither could Barkley.

Duran was like that. Cold. Calculating. Sometimes impossible to hurt. Always difficult, if not impossible, to stop. Roberto Duran was born in the slums of Panama City, a million seeming miles from nowhere, sometimes shining shoes or catching fish to survive. As the product of a tough, indifferent inner city, Duran had to fend for himself early, warding off scavengers and fighting back predator thugs in search of food or money. But Roberto Duran would soon capitalize on his wicked upbringing to become one of Panama's richest men, with worldwide fame, fortune and respect as he methodically pummeled one opponent upon another.

Sugar Ray Leonard was a smooth boxer under the tutelage of boxing legend Angelo Dundee who turned him into a seasoned puncher after his Olympic victory in 1976. By 1979 Sugar Ray had dropped Wilfredo Benitez to capture the professional welterweight crown and the following year, still early in his pro career, Leonard faced the menace called Roberto Duran. Taking a page from the taunts of Muhammad Ali, Duran worked on Leonard's ego and psyche before the fight, even telling Leonard's wife he was going to "keel" her husband. The result was predictable, as Ray was defeated both in and out of the ring by the street brawler Duran.

Manos de Piedra. Duran's nick name was "hands of stone," and he often showed why, possessing a string of sixty-nine victories in seventy fights, fifty-five by knockouts. With just a third grade education to go with a lifetime on the mean streets of Panama, a hungry Duran first stepped into the professional ring with a zest for violence at just 15 years of age. When he finally fought his way from the slums to the glitzy lights of Madison Square

Garden at the close of 1971, he was scorned as a skinny kid, a throw away item, even a fraudulent stiff—until he knocked his unsuspecting opponent Benny Huertas stone cold for six full minutes.

Almost ten years later Duran would fight Sugar Ray Leonard again, and this time the cagey Angelo Dundee told his protégé to box, box and run, box and hit—box a smart fight. Whether mentally or physically exhausted, or both, Duran was caught off guard and bludgeoned by the vengeful Leonard. Thoroughly defeated, the exhausted Duran struggled to save himself and, when that failed, he panicked into a full surrender. Two minutes and forty-four seconds into the eighth round, the legend of Roberto Duran was rewritten. "No mas!" came the capitulation of Duran. He wanted "no more," and his words echoed through the New Orleans Superdome, across state lines and beyond the seas as boxing's surrender heard round the world.

Duran would return to fight another day, even if his legend did not fully recover, and when he defeated Iran Barkely he actually won the middleweight title for the first time at age 37. But the last golden age of boxing was over in the early 1980's, never to surface again, even with the crushing victories of Mike Tyson and the nostalgic wins of an ageless George Foreman of the nineties. Much the way Sonny Liston failed to emerge for his next round with Muhammad Ali himself, Duran gave up—and with it he gave up the ghost of boxing's last noble era.

68 Steve Howe's Grievance

Steve Howe was a major league pitcher with problems galore. From 1982 to 1988 Howe was suspended by Major League Baseball and hospitalized for drug related treatments, each a half dozen times. The Major League drug policy traces its roots to Commissioner Peter Ueberroth, who prepared a policy memorandum placing drug monitoring and control under the purview of the commissioner's office, but the original policies were not tight with little guidance about random testing and other issues, setting the stage for a bizarre Baseball arbitration.

Because he violated his drug aftercare program, which was imposed for numerous prior drug incidents, Howe was again suspended during 1989 and 1990. On his behalf in 1990, the Players Association filed a grievance to get him back on the mound, and after Howe agreed to a battery of psychological and medical testing the commissioner permitted him to return, provided he comply with a tough new care program and submit to multiple random tests. Howe did return, and was tested regularly without incident. Howe proceeded to do well on the field, and in late 1991 signed a $2.3 million contract with the Yankees.

The good life lasted for almost exactly a month until Howe was arrested for attempted possession of cocaine, prompting then commissioner Fay Vincent to suspend Howe for life. The Players Association came to his aid again, contesting the ban in arbitration. The arbitrator's finding began on a low note for Howe, establishing this partial test for overturning a commissioner's decision:

> "As in any disciplinary matter, the burden of establishing just cause is on those imposing discipline. While the Commissioner has a 'reasonable range of discretion' in such matters, the penalty he imposes in a particular case must by 'reasonably commensurate with the offense' and appropriate, given all the circumstances."

According to the arbitrator's written opinion, the Commissioner justified the lifetime ban because Baseball had done all that could have been done and Howe had simply squandered the many chances Baseball had given him—a fairly reasonable position, it would seem. But the arbitrator had other concerns, differing with the Commissioner's interpretation, stating that "we now know that Howe has an underlying psychiatric disorder that was never diagnosed or treated; that this disorder has been a contributing factor to his use of drugs; and that, absent treatment for the condition, he remains vulnerable to such use."

The arbitrator also noted that although Baseball committed itself to random testing Howe often throughout the year, it failed to do so, thus setting Howe "on a course without the strategic safeguard [the doctor] consid-

73

ered indispensable to his success." The arbitrator begrudgingly conceded fault on Howe's part, but placed much of the blame on the commissioner and Baseball itself for failing to adhere to continuous testing. Said the arbitrator, "To give Howe yet another chance of returning to the game without implementing those conditions was not, in my judgment, a fair shot at success." Therefore, in 1992 Howe's lifetime suspension was reduced to time served to that point—119 days. Since players are not paid for absences due to suspension, Howe lost about $400,000 of his base salary, and the arbitrator felt that was enough.

The Steve Howe ordeal is a blunder of many faces, for it is difficult to tell who messed up the worst. Howe himself was suspended seven times for drug violations, including the lifetime ban, and was even arrested for attempted possession of cocaine along the way, a remarkable series of blunders brought on himself. Baseball screwed up by failing to administer the random testing that it made such a fuss about then, for whatever reason, blew the arbitration. And the arbitrator himself made a mockery of the system, invoking the ire of Commissioner Vincent who is quoted with this response:

"It's like saying you've had seven chances, but eight is the right number. How can there be soundness in that judgment? That makes the whole thing a joke. [The arbitrator] is saying he's giving him one more chance. Well, I did that in 1989."

The Howe case has had a significant impact upon sports, chilling league efforts to discipline players. It is extremely ironic, for normally players and the unions devote considerable effort fighting the concept of random testing, but Howe's arbitrator set them back twenty years by blaming Baseball for not testing Howe enough. Every time a commissioner in any sport considers a major penalty against a player, he has to consider the possibility of a Howe-type backlash. For example, if NBA Commissioner David Stern were ever to suspend the likes of a Dennis Rodman for a year or longer, he could almost count on a Steve Howe-like battle.

The Taunting Yost

About twenty-five miles due west of Chicago lies the tree lined, some-times lazy community of Wheaton, Illinois. In the midst of an era marked by ice cream socials, band concerts in the park and Model-T's chugging along main street, a young seventh grader was caught up in a neighborhood run-ning game loosely resembling today's football. He was athletic, inheriting the genes of his six-foot father who at one time was foreman of a lumberjack camp, occasionally impressing the workers with his own running acuity.

Less than ten years later the eager lad from Wheaton was a three-time all American football player at Illinois, a time when Big Ten and other major college football was king and the NFL was not much more than a glint in George Halas' eye. At that time Fielding Yost was the fabled coach of mighty Michigan, ranked in 1924 as the number one team in the country. He was as icon of major college coaches, and his Michigan Wolverines had a swagger in their walk and chips on their padded shoulders as they emerged from the stadium tunnel.

Little did Yost's team suspect their coach had already doomed them to posterity, having earlier invented one mien of contemporary American sports and planting the seeds of another: the taunt, followed by the almighty back-fire. Publicly dismissing [a verb; equivalent of "dissing" in nineties lingo] Illinois' great Red Grange as a football player, openly criticizing him with such taunts as "all he can do is run," Yost set in motion the turning tables of history.

An energized Grange listened and waited, biding time until he could demonstrate that little thing of his called running, plus a lot more. Grange exploded from the opening whistle, relentlessly churning up sod, chewing both turf and Wolverines as he plowed through, around and over the vaunted Michigan defense. Grange ran for one a touchdown, then another. And another and still another—four touchdowns in the first quarter alone!

Grange would run for another score bringing his total to five on the day, and specifically to prove Yost completely wrong Grange threw six pass completions including one for a touchdown, giving him a hand in six total touchdowns on the day. But his running was something special, gaining a staggering 402 yards on the ground himself as Illinois pummeled number one Michigan 39-14, adding to Grange's legend as the "galloping ghost" of the Fighting Illini from Champaign, Illinois.

By itself Yost's taunting had little significance in the scheme of history; and with or without it, Grange still had to do the running and make the scores. History can debate whether the taunting was instrumental in the dismantling of Michigan, or whether its significance was greater than other blunders such as those of Ben Johnson, the Hornsby trade, or the Dempsey-Tunney long count. But in the context of football history, considering that Grange would catch the eye of George Halas and eventually sign with the Bears to put pro football on the map for good, this one totally unnecessary indiscretion and Grange's rampage over Michigan were significant, combining to lift Illinois, knock off top rated Michigan, and lay the groundwork for the National Football League.

The Saga of Jim Thorpe's Medals

"He was the greatest athlete who ever lived. Lovely fellah. What he had was natural ability. There wasn't anything he couldn't do. All he had to see is someone doin' something and he tried it ... and he'd do it better. He had brute strength ... stamina ... endurance. A lot of times, like in the decathlon, he didn't know what he was doing. He didn't know the right way to throw the javelin or the discus but it didn't matter. He just went there and threw it further than anyone else."
—Abel Kiviat, silver medalist at the 1912 Olympic Games in Stockholm, recounting the wonder of Jim Thorpe seventy years later.

Jim Thorpe was a Native American born in Oklahoma, part Sac and Fox, part Potawatomie and Kickapoo. He had a little Irish and French blood, too, rendering him in some respects the consummate "melting pot" American. He also had a gift. One of his early coaches, the one and only "Pop" Warner, would write of Thorpe later: "He had speed as well as strength. He knew how to use his strength and speed as well as any football player or track athlete I have ever known."

The first time Jim Thorpe ever played football was in 1907 at the Carlisle Indian School. Four years later he beat Harvard University nearly by himself, scoring one touchdown and kicking four field goals for an 18-15 win. His greatest feats were yet to come, however, for only a year later he won both the decathlon and pentathlon at the 1912 Olympic Games in Stockholm, Sweden. Just winning the Olympic decathlon traditionally qualifies one as "the world's greatest athlete," but in 1912 a new modern pentathlon was introduced at the Games. Consisting of horse riding, fencing, swimming, shooting, and cross-country running, this new pentathlon tested a wide array of skills above and beyond the grueling track and field tests of the traditional decathlon. No matter to Thorpe; he simply won them both.

Only one year later, a stringent Olympic Committee learned through the Amateur Athletic Union that during the summer of 1909 a struggling Jim Thorpe had earned $25 per week playing minor league baseball. Thorpe was castigated and unceremoniously forced to return his Olympic medals. Forced out of the Olympics forever, Thorpe turned to pro football, playing for the Canton Bulldogs in 1915, leading them to championships in 1916, 1917 and 1919. He was a big draw, multiplying Canton crowds to nearly ten times the levels from before he arrived.

Just for good measure, Thorpe also played Major League Baseball for the New York Giants from 1913 to 1919 as an outfielder. His last season, at age 31, Thorpe batted .327 in 62 games.

Jim Thorpe died in 1953, just short of his 65th birthday, an event that triggered a groundswell of support for reinstating his Olympic medals earned forty-one years before. The U.S. Olympic Committee finally relented in 1982, and on January 18, 1983, Jim Thorpe's medals were again presented, this time to his children.

For the better part of the twentieth century the U.S. Olympic Committee was at war with American athletes, sniffing out hints of professionalism as though earning a living were a crime. The authorities were probably delighted to do a hatchet job on Thorpe, but in so doing they altered Olympic history, contributed to the success of pro football in America, and sent a pretty good outfielder to the New York Giants. More recently the Committee learned that paranoid cruelty is unproductive and archaic, allowing professionals to compete as human beings, not criminals. Too bad they weren't big enough to do that in 1913.

The Giants Dump Hack Wilson

Hack Wilson was a hard hitting major leaguer who loved kids, signed autographs, set the National League record for both home runs (56) and RBI's (190)—and was a prolific drunk. He retired in 1934 and died a pauper in 1948, at age 48. Only his drinking kept Lewis Robert Wilson out of the Hall of Fame until 1979, a shame, if not a blunder in its own right, considering all the shenanigans of other athletes over the years.

Wilson was a peculiar ball player. He was only 5'6" tall and weighed over 200 pounds, packing a compact, powerful swing. Highlighting his top-heavy power, Hack had a size 18 collar and only a size 6 shoe, almost "Quasimoto" dimensions and, according to some, his nickname "Hack" may have come from George Hackenschmidt, a bulky wrestler with similar "no-neck" proportions.

The record setting Wilson was originally a New York Giant, but they dumped him in 1924 after he hit .239, relegating him to a Toledo minor league team. In a player draft after the season, the Chicago Cubs picked Wilson up for a song—$5,000 cash. The Giants mounted a protest, but this only telegraphed their true desire to keep Wilson and aggravated their blunder, but their pleas were to no avail as Commissioner Kennesaw Mountain Landis rejected them as too late. Hack Wilson went on to bat cleanup for the Cubs, smashing hits, homers and RBI's at record paces. He had hitting streaks of 25 and 27 games; in 1930 he had a phenomenal full season slugging percentage of .723; and during his record RBI year, Wilson batted in 53 runs in August alone!

After 1930 Hack began to slump again, liquor and a lack of focus catching up, but not before setting records that would last more than 60 years and counting. The Giants blew it; they could have had Wilson and his RBI's and other records all to themselves. It was worse than just not signing a superstar because the price tag was too high, such as the Cleveland Indians did when they let Albert Belle go before the 1997 season because of the monster money he required. Cleveland's miscue was bad enough, but to lose a player of similar, if not greater proportions for a measly $5,000 just by failing to protect him properly was more than a mistake, it was a sports blunder that shaped the next six years of Baseball and the National League record books altogether.

The Munich Hostages

The 1972 Summer Olympic Game were contaminated by terrorist acts of cowardice that took the lives of Israeli athletes at the Olympic village compound. If ranked for sheer stupidity alone, these criminal transgressions would rate at or near the top of our sports blunder list. The rank assigned, however, reflects two mitigating factors for purposes of our definition: First, the Olympics recovered nicely, both in 1972 and subsequent years, these acts of terrorism being relegated to what they truly were—an isolated crime. Second, they weren't entirely sports decisions, per se, although they certainly were intertwined with sports and there is little doubt the Olympics were specifically targeted for their international visibility.

To place the 1972 games in context, they brought the seven gold medals of Mark Spitz, the electrifying performance of Russian gymnast Olga Korbut, five medals for female Australian swimmer Shane Gould (three of them gold), and the expulsion of Rhodesia for apartheid politics. But of course the Munich Olympics are infamous in sports history for one salient reason and one alone: a kidnapping attempt by Palestinian guerrillas on Israel's Olympic team, resulting in eleven dead athletes along with five terrorists and one policeman killed during a rescue attempt.

A twisted assault upon the Olympic ideal. (UPI/Corbis-Bettmann)

Four years later, at the Montreal Olympics, security was extremely tight and the Israeli Olympic team wore black armbands in memory of their fallen comrades from Munich as the 1976 games continued without violence or terrorism.

Notre Dame and Gerry Faust

What was Notre Dame thinking?

To begin at the end, Notre Dame football coach Gerry Faust had this to say after his tenure with the Fighting Irish: "Notre Dame never would have fired me. I resigned because I felt I needed a fresh start and Notre Dame needed a fresh start." His reflective words were hardly an endorsement of Faust's own football program in South Bend, and it appears someone made one or more sports blunders in sentencing Notre Dame to a half-decade of mediocrity before landing Lou Holtz. How?

Gerry Faust seemingly came out of nowhere when he landed the Notre Dame job. To be fair, although he was just a high school football coach, Faust's teams did have an extraordinary record of achievement for Catholic Moeller High School in Cincinnati, Ohio, going 174-17-2. In 71 games from 1975 through 1980, his Moeller teams won five state championships and four hypothetically bestowed national titles. Not bad at all, so what went wrong at Notre Dame?

As good a Faust's records were, his amazing high school achievements in hindsight did not, and logically could not, have translated well at Notre Dame. According to South Bend sportswriters, Faust was unable to work well with college assistant coaches he inherited, and as he weeded them out he did not or could not find first-rate replacements. According to published reports, some of the players had difficulty, too, complaining he treated them more as high schoolers than big time college or "pro caliber" athletes.

When Faust departed Notre Dame in 1985, he landed at Akron where he began to spend vast sums of athletic department money, plunging it into a $585,000 deficit in his first six months. He then managed to play a Division I-AA schedule and achieved a progressively worsening record, going 5-6 in 1988, including a spectacular loss to Auburn (42-0) and losing also to lowly I-AA Arkansas State, all of which inspired the *Sporting News* to rate Akron as the worst program among all Division I-A schools.

How Faust crashed from the heights of high school coaching to the lowest depths of sub-mediocrity at the college level may never be fully understood, but the primary reason may very well have been very simple: he was in the right place at the right time in Moeller High. Was the Peter Principle at work, finally elevating Faust to an ultimate level of incompetence? Regardless of the reason, Notre Dame should have known better. Sure, Faust's Moeller record must have been enticing, but he had absolutely no college level experience—even as an assistant coach, not at any level, such as I-AA, let alone Division I, not to mention one of the most high profile pressure cooker jobs in college football: Notre Dame.

Unable to recruit for or effectively coach the demanding Notre Dame program, Faust finally faded away to Division I-A Akron, leaving the once invincible Fighting Irish awash in a wake of mediocrity.

62 NFL Blackouts

In 1961 Congress enacted the federal Sports Broadcasting Act, essentially making it legal to monopolize pro sports telecasts. Combined with its antitrust implications and some remarkable back scratching between the NFL and key members of Congress, the Act was a sports blunder making the top twenty of our list all on its own.

The Act made it possible for teams to "blackout" their home games, keeping them from television even though others, perhaps the whole country, could watch. In essence, Congress gave the leagues the right to be dumb (one blunder), and at least one—the NFL—was quick to oblige (another blunder). Although the value of television was obvious, especially to leagues such as the NFL, pro football nonetheless waged a war with its fans to keep non-sellouts off TV. Certainly the NFL has always desired to fill football stadiums, but the question is at what price?

For example, in 1962 the NFL blacked out the championship game between the Chicago Bears and the New York Giants. Neither fans in Chicago nor New York could see the game! Not only were the two biggest television markets in the country erased, they were the home teams in the championship, certainly capable of drawing the highest proportion of viewers by a wide margin. Fans were furious, even to the extent of filing a lawsuit in New York to enjoin the blackout, alleging that whatever restrictions were allowable under the Sports Broadcasting Act during the regular season did not apply to post-season play. The court was not amused, upholding the blackout and affirming the NFL's right to shoot itself in the foot, but the emotional pain of the fans was evident by their heartfelt, though awkward legal argument that the "deprivation of their right to observe (the game on TV) in common with the millions of Americans to whom it is being televised is a violation of a basic human right, guaranteed by the Constitution and the law of the land."

The NFL could not even argue its blackouts rationally applied *only* to non-sellouts—because they *didn't*. It even blacked out most of the early Super Bowls, spawning numerous rounds of lawsuits by irate fans. What was the logical purpose of denying a sold out Superbowl game to local fans? The NFL won these cases, but it caught the negative attention of Congress— no doubt in part due to hostile fans calling their local representatives—and relented, begrudgingly showing Super Bowl VII in 1973. Congress intervened anyway, passing a federal law prohibiting the blackout of any local game that was sold out at least 72 hours in advance. That legislation expired at the end of 1975, but the NFL has voluntarily adhered to the 72-hour rule ever since.

A case could—should?—be made that the NFL is nonetheless ill-advised to continue blackouts under any conditions. First, other leagues have relatively few, if any, restrictions. Baseball does not blackout its games, rather Baseball shows as much on TV as possible—especially in cities sporting superstations such as Chicago, New York and Atlanta. If Baseball failed to show games on TV, it might force a few more fans into the stadiums, but it would drop out of sight in the public eye, cutting off its nose (and broadcast revenue) to spite its television face. Hockey, meanwhile, would love to have a TV contract for greater revenue and exposure, and blacking out games would be the last thing it would do if it had a television deal. Even the wildly successful NBA does not arrogantly punish its fans by yanking games from non-sellout cities. Television rules: Nike commercials, beer, NBA merchandise, cars and automotive supplies are bombarded to millions of fans, and the last thing a league should do is yank the rug on games because some fans fail to attend in person. A full stadium is nothing compared to the television extravaganza, and fan support and loyalty should be nurtured, especially when a team fan base extends well beyond city limits into outer suburbia. If a team is poor, the suburban fans won't flock to distant venues whether the game is on TV or not, and if the team is good both the stadium and the airwaves are engulfed by fan interest.

Further, in this day and age of "free agent franchises" where unsuccessful teams readily pack up and move, fan punishment to force stadium attendance is superfluous, if not counterproductive. The best way to get fans into the stadium is to provide a good product and televise it, for TV games are one giant commercial for the in-person entertainment value offered. If teams don't draw fans over the long haul, they simply bolt for another city. Thus, the NFL blackout rule is itself counterproductive and ill-advised even today, and when it was implemented and utilized to black out even Super Bowl games it was sheer lunacy, wreaking havoc on the sports community and in the courts for years.

The Kermit Washington/Rudy Tomjanovich Superbout

With their high intensity, lightning fast athletes and relentless physical contact, the leading professional team sports are potential breading grounds for sudden on-court violence. These dangers are as real in basketball and football as they are in the seemingly gentile world of baseball (although on this topic hockey is on another planet), and as the stakes get higher and the athletes stronger, the potential hotbed gets even worse.

Sports violence, however, is not a new phenomenon. In 1905 President Theodore Roosevelt threatened to use the Presidency to outlaw football altogether when an unsettled University of Pennsylvania team nearly killed an opposing lineman from Swarthmore, highlighting the fact that nearly twenty deaths a year were occurring in college football games just after the turn of the century. Instead, the major universities got together and agreed to outlaw certain tactics, such as the flying wedge, and after much internal strife and posturing these conferences evolved into the National Collegiate Athletic Association; hence, the NCAA was originally created as a safety monitoring devise to regulate on-field sports conduct.

One could pick any one of hundreds of on-field episodes of violence as a sports blunder. For example, in 1973 "Booby" Clark of the NFL Bengals blasted Denver Broncos player Dale Hackbart in the back with an illegal hit causing a broken vertebrae, muscular atrophy and loss of reflexes in his arm, prompting Hackbart to sue Clark. More notably, self-proclaimed assassin

Jack Tatum, an Oakland Raiders defensive back, hit Patriots receiver Darryl Stingley with enough force to permanently paralyze Stingley. In a 1969 hockey incident Wayne Maki of the St. Louis Blues cracked Boston player Ted Green with a hockey stick, fracturing Green's skull and causing massive hemorrhaging.

In the late 1980's and early 1990's the author was one of the attorneys for Chicago Bear star quarterback Jim McMahon, who had a competitive knack for bringing out the worst in opposing defensive players, and I distinctly remember his televised on-field incident with Packer Charles Martin in 1986. With the Bears on offense, QB McMahon drifted toward the sidelines as he gazed ahead watching the end of a play. After the play, Green Bay's Charles Martin blind-sided Jim from behind, lifted him bear-hug style and slammed his tender shoulder down on the hard turf, knocking Jim out of the game. Jim missed the rest of the 1986 season, a significant year since the Bears were attempting to repeat their dominating Super Bowl victory following the 1985 season. The Bears would go 14-2, barely missing a second straight Super Bowl—a trip they likely would have made with a healthy Jim McMahon.

Jim had experienced pain and great difficulty with his shoulder from prior injuries, and Charles Martin and the whole NFL community was aware of Jim's plight. Even so, Martin entered the game with a "hit list" of numbers on the towel he wore at belt level, including Jim's own #9. I felt Jim had a legitimate claim and should have considered a lawsuit, but ultimately no legal action was taken. This may have been the smart choice since Jim kept right on playing for ten more years, ironically finishing his career with the Packers and capturing one more Super Bowl ring from the 1996 championship season. Martin, by the way, was suspended by the league offices for two games, and eventually dropped out of the game, becoming little more than an NFL afterthought

But the "Super Bowl" of stupidity for on-court violence may have been the brutal attack by the Lakers' Kermit Washington's on Rudy Tomjanovich of the Rockets (who later would lead Houston to two world titles as coach during the Michael Jordan baseball hiatus) during a fight in the midst of a 1977 NBA game. Rudy "T" was rewarded with a concussion, fractures to his nose, jaw and skull, facial lacerations, severe loss of blood and leakage of spinal fluid from the brain cavity. Washington was suspended for a record number of games and the Lakers were promptly sued by Tomjanovich, who had to climb over some legal hurdles known as "assumption of the risk," a principle that prevents players from suing each other for injuries on the court. One of his theories was negligent hiring, alleging that the Lakers, as Kermit's employer, knew him to be a violent player and that the club was negligent in its hiring, training and supervising of him.

The Lakers defended the case, which went all the way to a jury verdict, invoking an argument of self-defense on Washington's part. The jury didn't buy it and awarded Tomjanovich $3.25 million, after which the case was settled for an undisclosed amount.

Kermit Washington's attack was not only vicious, it symbolized a new era of violence in sports—and is unique as one of the few victories by injured athletes against opposing players and, in this case, a team. Had Jim McMahon sued the Green Bay Packers under a similar theory could he have won? Under the circumstances of Martin's towel hit list and related conduct, such would be a logical outcome. As it is, the Kermit Washington incident has become an unofficial standard of aberrant conduct against which other transgressions are measured. For example, when Chicago Bull Dennis Rodman's kicking incident drew a suspension of eleven games it was promptly compared to and measured against the Kermit Washington attack.

CHAPTER FIVE:
Happy (?) Endings

Muhammad Ali's Last Fight

Muhammad Ali was a showman. He loved life, verbally jousting with other people, and he loved being a fighter. When Ali was in training for the second Liston fight in 1965, he barked out to a young reporter, "If I said I would knock out Sonny Liston in one minute and forty-nine seconds of the first round, it would hurt the gate." As it happened Ali would knock the monster Liston out in one minute fifty-two seconds.

Ali was one of few people to actually achieve legend status in his own time, stinging opponents in the ring and relentlessly toying with their egos, sometimes assigning nicknames such as the Gorilla (Joe Frazier), the Mummy (George Foreman) and the Bear (Sonny Liston). And the fire in Ali's eyes, his competitive spirit and insatiable desire to win and win again may have been his ultimate strength, a tenacity seen in few others, most recently by the intense eyes of Michael Jordan when he drifts into one of his unstoppable "zones" on the court.

But if a person desires to assess his weaknesses, he need only list his greatest strengths, for they are the same. Ali's iron will, for example, would not let him lose. It also would not let him quit until it was too late—and so goes the story of Muhammad's last fight.

With middleweight speed and heavyweight power, a youthful Cassius Clay would one day rewrite boxing history.
(UPI/Corbis-Bettmann)

Some observers saw Ali as prone to self-destruction, including his long time fight doctor Ferdie Pacheco who noted as much in his insightful 1992 book recounting Ali's escapades, including all the unpopular and therefore dangerous choices he made from turning Muslim on the eve of his first Sonny Liston fight in 1964 to his famous battle with the draft board only a few years later. But Ali was an emotional man, so he may have just been following inner voices that compelled him to follow his gut. Or maybe he just couldn't resist toying with fate, giving himself competitive roadblocks much the way he taunted and toyed with the competition his whole career.

Ali's last fight symbolized his unwillingness to give up, his zest for competition and above all winning—not to mention the limelight. But a careful review of posterity suggests Ali's last fight occurred at least five different times!—a quirk of fate that only Ali the showman could muster. His first "last" fight, only three years after defeating Liston for the title, was against Zora Folley on March 22, 1967, in New York, after which Ali refused induction into the armed forces and was stripped of his title. Under the circumstances of the times, it certainly appeared his final bout had at last been fought, and by all rights it very well could have been.

It appeared grim enough in February of 1970 for Ali to announce his retirement, but Ali the magician conquered fate, battling back in the Supreme Court of the United States and regaining his right to fight in the ring, defeating Jerry Quarry by technical knockout in the third round on October 26, 1970. Ali fought on, losing only twice over the next seven years (Joe Frazier in 1971 and Ken Norton in 1973) in twenty-seven fights, with no losses at all in 1974, 1975 and 1976. Then came Leon Spinks on February 15, 1978, when at 36 years of age time had seemingly caught up and Ali lost his title again, this time by a fifteen round decision.

By all logic, Ali's last fight could have, would have, should have been the Spinks loss, for how many fighters could successfully come back after losing the title at age 36? But no, not for the strong willed Muhammad. He fought Spinks in a rematch on September 15, 1978, this time winning a fifteen round decision to regain the world heavyweight title. Then he did just what the pundits would approve: Ali announced his retirement on June 27, 1979.

If Ali fooled the rest of the world, he did not fool himself. He failed to stay retired for long, coming back to fight Larry Holmes in a match to win a then vacant title slot on October 2, 1980. A listless Ali struggled through the fight, a mere punching bag for his former sparring partner Holmes, finally giving up at the eleventh round. For all practical purposes this was in fact Ali's last fight, his fourth "last" as it were.

But there would be one more over a year later, assuming one could call it a fight. One month short of his fortieth birthday Ali took on Trevor Berbick in Nassau, losing an ugly fight in ten rounds. The match was an especially foul exercise. As Ali's great trainer Angelo Dundee recounted, there was no fight bell and they had to employ an old fashioned cow bell instead; the boxing gloves were lost; and Ali himself was way overweight.

Many of Ali's supposed last fights might be considered a blunder, and so could each fight following each blunder match. But the one that symbolically represented the worst of the bunch, and a fight that would portend the precarious fate of Ali in later years, was probably the Larry Holmes disaster. As early as 1977 lab reports showed Ali's kidneys were deteriorating. Those close to him noticed a distinct difference in his walk and speech. The Las Vegas Boxing Commission insisted on a complete physical exam in advance of the 1980 Holmes fight, which Ali passed at the Mayo Clinic. But his one time fight doctor Ferdie Pacheco, who lost control over Ali in the legendary boxer's latter fight years, had reservations. For one, Ali was indeed in good shape for many 38-year-olds, at least by all normal appearances and standard medical tests. Second, Ali charmed the doctors at Mayo clinic and probably appeared witty, sharp and in control—again, compared to normal people. But no normal people were about to enter the ring against a wicked puncher and superlative fighting machine like Larry Holmes. His good reflexes were the equivalent of bad reflexes; under those circumstances good is not good enough, and even great is only adequate.

One test that did produce an interesting result showed no evidence of low blood sugar or low thyroid function, both of which were thought to be diagnosed in Ali before the Zaire fight in 1974. The problem lay not with the newer Mayo tests but with the treatment stemming from the old ones. Treating Ali for low thyroid when he had no such condition could have been, and may very well have created, a dangerous condition. According to published accounts of Dr. Pacheco, the do-gooder entourage that hung over Ali during the latter part of his career squeezed out Pacheco and subjected Ali to a round of diets, supplements, colonic irrigations and other counterproductive measures.

Preceding the Holmes encounter, Ali had ballooned up to massive physical proportions. In a desperate, ill-advised effort to resurrect his distant past, Ali made the final blunder of using amphetamines to help him not only lose weight quickly, but to get down to his 1964 weight of 210 pounds. By this time Percheco was no longer around to advise a 38-year-old boxer of the dangers associated with artificially losing weight, especially to levels no longer consistent with an individual's age and natural body weight. In short, then, Ali entered the fight in a highly weakened state.

If that were not enough, as the fight itself wore on Holmes got stronger and dominated Ali at will, even to the point where Holmes himself looked to the referee for mercy, pleading for a stoppage of the fight with ever saddening eyes. But the embattled Ali would not go down; just as he beat Foreman when he should not have, just as he defeated the entire United States military establishment, and just as he had pummeled the unbeatable Liston sixteen years before and the even more unbeatable George Forman in Zaire, the determined Ali hung tough, leaning on the ropes, absorbing the reluctant fists of Larry Holmes, doing whatever necessary to remain standing. But by the eleventh round Muhammad's best friend and confidant Herbert Muhammad had finally had enough, throwing in the towel. The fight, and for all practical purposes Ali's career, were finally over.

Had the audacious, lovable, hatable, loud, emotional, proud, invincible competitor Ali remained retired in 1979 after winning the title back in his Spinks rematch, perhaps the world would still be reeling from the wild antics of an energetic Ali the statesman. Instead we are left with a living legend, demur, battered, but still proud, defeated physically but not in spirit.

Were that it not be so.

Dismantling the 1985 Bears

Although the storied Chicago Bears had won championships over the years, they only went to the Super Bowl once, winning in grand fashion after a monster 1985 season with fifteen wins and only one loss, not counting three stunning post-season victories with combined scores over New York, Los Angeles and New England of 91-10, including two consecutive shutouts.

With a punishing ground attack and dependable passing game, the Bears offense was led by Walter Payton, Jim McMahon, Wille Gault and Dennis McKinnon, with Matt Suhey at fullback and an all-pro offensive line. As good as the offense was, it was surpassed in excitement by the defense, possibly the best defense ever to play the game of football. Behind the crusty genius of defensive coordinator Buddy Ryan, the 1985 defense not only beat teams on its own, it beat them up in the process, sometimes changing opponent teams for years to come like when the Cowboys were destroyed 44-0 in Dallas, the first Cowboys shutout in 218 games and worst overall defeat in Dallas history.

Ironically the Bears began the season with a lackluster first half at home against a weak Tampa Bay team, falling behind 28-17 by half-time, after which the Bears rebounded to win 38-28, never looking back with a defensive roster of all-pro caliber players: Dan Hampton (LE); Steve McMichael

(LT); William "Refrigerator" Perry (RT); Richard Dent (RE); Otis Wilson (LB); Mike Singletary (LB); Wilber Marshall (LB); Leslie Frazier (CB); Gary Fencik (FS); and Dave Duerson (SS). Two defensive standouts, Al Harris and Todd Bell, were contract holdouts in 1985, but both still were named to the Bear all-defensive team of the 1980's. Not only was the defense stingy with points, it registered three safeties and rolled up quarterback sacks with reckless abandon, including six against the Giants in the playoffs and seven more against the Patriots in the Super Bowl. The Bears broke five Super Bowl records, including 21 points in the third quarter, most points scored, and largest margin of victory.

In 1986 the Bears followed their stellar performance by going 14-2 and setting an NFL record of fewest points allowed in a season: 187 points over 16 games, an average of only 11.7 per game. But problems had begun to surface, as defensive coordinator Buddy Ryan was already gone and the players, though still doing well, complained it was harder to register sacks and to control opposing offenses—they were still succeeding but it was taking a physical toll. On offense Jim McMahon got hurt, Walter Payton lost a step, and they lost to the Redskins in the playoffs at home 27-13.

As the years passed, many of the stellar performers were let go: Willie Gault, Wilber Marshall, Richard Dent, Jay Hilgenberg, Jim McMahon and others. Combined with retirements and injuries, these personnel moves slowly dismantled the team, and the vaunted Super Bowl Bears eventually fell apart until the team collapsed completely in 1989 with a frustrating losing record of 6-10. Not only did the Bears let free agents walk out the door, they were slow to react to the positive side of free agency, failing to plug holes as they developed or draft wisely to replace injured and retired veterans.

The 1985 Bears may not have been the best team ever overall (although their defense probably was the best to suit up), they likely were the best never to regain an appearance in the Super Bowl. Over a 3-year span they would go 40-7, but never reach the final game again. By the end of 1992 even their icon coach Mike Ditka would be gone. (When punky, but gutsy quarterback Jim McMahon was let go he vowed to win another Super Bowl ring before Mike Ditka. He did, but not until he coasted in as a back-up on the 1996 Super Bowl Packers. The fired Ditka, meanwhile, would be out of coaching until landing the New Orleans job in 1997.) Had the 1985 Bears remained intact, could they have become the "first" Chicago Bulls by winning back to back to back titles? Perhaps. Perhaps not. But it is likely the dismantling of the team radically changed the course of Bear history and that of all professional football for a number of years to come.

58 Dallas-Minnesota Blockbuster Trade

A superb athlete whose efforts would shame even many Olympians, Herschel J. Walker not only rushed for 6,137 yards in his high school football career, he won the Georgia state shot-put championship plus two sprinting events. As a freshman running back at the University of Georgia, Herschel set an NCAA freshman record with 1,616 yards, earning All-American status and placing an astonishing third in the Heisman Trophy voting. If that were not enough, in both his freshman and sophomore years at Georgia, Walker was All-American in track, too.

Passing up his senior year, the unstoppable Walker signed on with the New Jersey Generals in 1983, helping to launch the United States Football League to competitive prominence against the entrenched NFL. True to form, he led the USFL in rushing yards and in rushing touchdowns.

Two years later in 1985, the NFL Dallas Cowboys would go up against the bone crushing Chicago Bears of Hampton, Perry, Dent, McMichael, Singletary, Wilson, and Marshall. Even though the game was in Dallas, the Bear defense demolished the Cowboys line, quarterback, receivers—everybody, in a 44-0 bloodbath that would rock the once proud Cowboys back on their heels all the way from the offensive line to the front office. One year later the Cowboys, desperate to rejuvenate quickly, signed the invincible Herschel Walker and made him the highest paid running back in NFL history. Walker lived up to his billing at times, but the Cowboys just weren't good enough yet as a team to utilize him properly. Their overall strength, experience and team speed were still lacking, and by 1989 they were determined to make a change.

So were the Minnesota Vikings, who sent six players and twelve draft choices to Dallas for Herschel Walker! Minnesota general manager Mike Lynn publicly predicted the stunning blockbuster trade would bring a Super Bowl. It did—for Dallas.

Remarkably, Herschel's explosive, improvising power game did not fit the Minnesota offense which relied more on finesse at the time. Walker was released, going to the Eagles where he again excelled. Meanwhile, Dallas used the plethora of players and draft choices to put the finishing touches on its 1990's dynasty-in-the-making under a run led by coach Jimmy Johnson.

The Fog Bowl

Immediately following the 1988 regular season the Chicago Bears met Philadelphia for a first-round playoff game in Chicago's Soldier Field. It was a beautiful day, sunny and unseasonably mild for winter in the Windy City. The author was at the game, soaking up the sky's low sun when an eerie cloud rolled over the south and west walls of the stadium while the game was in full progress. As the puffy white haze poured down the stands and onto the field it was a sight from outer space.

A wind shift propelled the lingering mist eastward from cold Lake Michigan waters, engulfing the stadium. In a matter of several minutes the sun was gone and a cold fog stubbornly replaced the Indian Summer warmth with an icy, dark blanket causing the entire field, the ball, the players and the officials to completely disappear! The television cameras caught only the gray-lined interior of the fog layer, turning everyone's screen a useless off-white void. The announcers could not see the game at all, so their play-by-play call was impossible. The players had difficulty seeing each other, officials could see little of the field—and yet the game went on! A playoff game with sudden death significance not only was played in impossible conditions, it was televised to the end. Occasionally fans in the stadium could see a jersey, then maybe two or three, emerge from the fog, usually as tacklers rode an offensive player out of bounds. Then they would all disappear back into the mist, not to be seen for several plays.

The Bears, who won the game 20-12, may indeed have been the better team with home field advantage and a 1988 record of 13-5 (including playoffs), but their alleged superiority was not a given by any means. The Eagles had come to town with a winning record, fresh off consecutive victories over Phoenix and Dallas, sporting such NFL stars as Randall Cunningham, Keith Byars, Keith Jackson, Cris Carter, Eric Allen and Reggie White. But if playing the Bears in Chicago were not hard enough, the intense fog probably favored the Bears, helping influence the game outcome. While the Eagles relied upon a mobile quarterback in Cunningham, who loved to scramble and improvise plays by spotting receivers downfield, the Bears rolled out a wicked ground attack behind a pro-bowl offensive line, running Neal Anderson and Dennis Gentry down the gut. The fog played havoc with Cunningham's wide open offense, favoring the conservative Bears.

The game did not profoundly affect the history of the NFL, and it probably had no outcome on the Super Bowl, because the Bears went on to be defeated by San Francisco 28-3, a team that likely would have beaten the Eagles as well. But weighted on sheer stupidity, continuing the game was a gross blunder, as was televising it to an audience that couldn't see a thing. Because of its less than profound consequences, the game fails to rank in the top 50, but it nonetheless deserves mention as a contemporary example of how anything that can go wrong will—and be tolerated by otherwise intelligent referees, league officials and network executives.

Franchise Free Agents: The Wayward Raiders

The Oakland-Los Angeles-Oakland Raiders and their colorful, enigmatic owner Al Davis waged the "super bowl" of sports litigation warfare during the 1980's, and it all started with Los Angeles Rams owner Carroll Rosenbloom.

In 1978 the City of Anaheim began luring the Rams from the L.A. Coliseum with an attractive stadium deal, while at the same time the Raiders were running into roadblocks in their own negotiations with the Oakland Coliseum. Rosenbloom did, in fact, move the Rams to Anaheim, in effect pushing over the first domino in a series of events that helped establish the "franchise free agency" that has developed today. The first domino was a lawsuit filed by the Los Angeles Coliseum against the NFL in 1978.

Davis, of course, decided to abandon Oakland for L.A., an especially significant move because NFL rules defined home territory as an area within a 75 mile radius of a given team's home base. Thus, the home territory of the new Anaheim Rams extended into and throughout Los Angeles, causing a required three-fourths vote of all NFL teams to approve the Raiders' move into the L.A. Coliseum. The rogue Davis did not fare well in the 1980 vote, the Raiders losing by a tally of 22 against the move, 0 in favor, with five teams abstaining, including the Rams, resulting in the Raiders joining the 1978 lawsuit already on file by the Coliseum. The Oakland Coliseum also intervened as a party creating a four-way donnybrook among the two Coliseums, the Raiders and the NFL, resulting in an federal antitrust jury trial in Los Angeles. The jury could not reach a final conclusion as to the reasonableness of the NFL rules and their antitrust implications, so a mistrial was declared and the parties started all over again. In a second trial on the same issues, the jury found antitrust violations and the NFL lost, appealing to the U.S. Court of Appeals where it lost again.

After two jury trials and one appeal, the Raiders odyssey was only beginning. Another trial was held just on the issue of damages to the Raiders, where a jury awarded the Raiders $11.5 million in lost profits (multiplied by three, as antitrust damages are normally trebled) for two years during their delay in moving south. But that decision was appealed, too, because the Raiders were deemed more valuable in Los Angeles than in Oakland.

But the courts and the Raiders were still far from finished. In 1982 the Raiders were hit in the north by Oakland itself in an effort to block the Los Angeles move, with Oakland attempting to "condemn" the Raiders and con-

fiscate them by eminent domain powers the same was a city would condemn an old factory to clear the way for a new highway. Condemn a football team? It's not so far fetched, for eminent domain laws need not just
apply to real estate; they can be invoked against any type of property, provided there is a legitimate public use and ample value is given for the confis-
cated property. But it also raises Constitutional questions, for if the condem-
nation unduly interferes with interstate commerce, the courts will strike it
down—this is one reason that Battle Creek, Michigan, would have difficulty
trying to "condemn" and keep Kellogg's, for example.

The Raiders lost the first round in the trial court, and the appellate
court reversed. The Raiders then raised Constitutional questions, which
were appealed again and eventually affirmed by the California Supreme
Court, preventing the City of Oakland from confiscating the Raiders, such
being a violation of the commerce clause of the U.S. Constitution.

All the Raiders litigation extended approximately eight years, start to
finish, and it resulted in the Raiders moving to L.A. after all. The Raiders
were not the first pro franchise to move (just ask Brooklyn), but they did
pave the way for franchise free agency even in the face of considerable legal
opposition. The move to L.A. was remarkably ill-conceived, in retrospect,
for the Raiders left a ravenous fan base in Oakland for the laid back, weak
support of Los Angeles fans who never fully backed the team. After all that,
the prodigal Raiders eventually packed up and moved back to Oakland,
completing their full circle of sports blunders.

Gretzky Bolts Edmonton

Mere greatness eludes hockey's Gretzky, for he transcends greatness
beyond almost all measure.

He became a pro at only age 16, played in the minors for two years and
then the World Hockey Association Indianapolis Racers, where he played
only eight games before being traded to the Edmonton Oilers. Had Gretzky
been somewhat more established at the time, this trade would make the

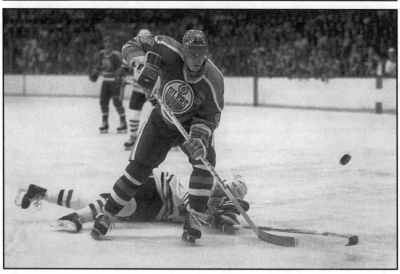

The "Great One" would skate his way through the record books from Edmonton to Los Angeles. (UPI/Corbis-Bettmann)

blunder list, too, for at Edmonton he simply went on to become the league rookie of the year. Gretzky landed in the NHL when the old WHA folded, where he won an astonishing eight straight scoring titles. He would have won nine in a row, but he suffered a knee injury in 1987-88 (but he still scored a whopping 149 points).

Although Gretzky "owned" Edmonton, he announced displeasure with the team and demanded out in 1988. The Oilers obliged, shipping him to the L.A. Kings for four players, three draft choices and a reported $15 million in cash. But not only was Edmonton devastated, the entire country of Canada was dealt a blow. His very first shot in a Kings uniform scored a goal; and in his first year the Kings defeated the Oilers in a dramatic, ironic seven game series. The great Gretzky went on to be the top scorer again in 1990 and 1991, and won the MVP award again in 1989, leaving a wake of seemingly endless NHL records, including: most career points, goals and assists; plus most points in a season, most season goals and season assists. In all he would break or tie fifty-three official NHL scoring records, many while a member of the L.A. Kings.

Warriors Dump Chamberlain

Wilt Chamberlain reinvented basketball, a remarkable feat for a young man who never played the sport until he was in seventh grade. A growth spurt took him to 6-feet 11 inches by the time he hit Overbrook High School in Philadelphia where his teams won three public school championships and two all-city titles.

Heavily recruited out of high school, Wilt landed at the University of Kansas, scoring 52 points in his first game (against Northwestern University). Reconfigured defenses kept him from matching that lofty total in college, but he did average 29.9 points and 18.3 rebounds in his career. Few fans now realize that Wilt left Kansas after his junior year, joining the Harlem Globetrotters for one season, before he signed on with the Philadelphia Warriors of the NBA in 1959. The Warriors had obtained special permission to claim his draft rights directly from high school in 1955, waiting four years to sign him as part of the dispensation. By this time Chamberlain was 7'2" and 300 pounds—a little taller than Shaquille O'Neal, for example—and in 1959 he dwarfed even the best of his NBA rivals. Wilt would break eight NBA records in his first year, including a 37.6 points per game average, winning both the Rookie of the Year award *and* league MVP.

When the Warriors left Philadelphia for San Francisco in 1962, Wilt went along and played until the middle of the 1965 season when the Warriors traded him to the Philadelphia 76ers. At least one published source awards this the worst trade in Warriors history (even worse than trading Robert Parish and a draft choice that became Kevin McHale to the Celtics for Joe Barry Carroll), and it would appear this is also one of the top sports blunders in all of basketball. Wilt Chamberlain was not a speculation, and he was not just a star—he *was* the NBA, and he was still very much in his prime. All the Warriors got for him were Connie Dierking, Paul Newman (not the actor, but that would have been better), Lee Schaffer and some cash.

Chamberlain had many fabled battles with Bill Russell and the Boston Celtics, but his teams lost to Boston five times in the championships until Chamberlain prevailed in 1967. Demonstrating remarkable versatility, Wilt modified his game in 1967, developing a low post passing game to take advantage of all the double teams thrown his way to lead the NBA in assists—the only center ever to do so. His athleticism should have been no surprise. While at Kansas he won the Big Eight high jumping title three straight years, put the shot 56 feet, and ran a 10.9 hundred yard dash.

By 1968 Wilt was traded again, this time to the Los Angeles Lakers where once more he reinvented himself, winning another NBA championship alongside Elgin Baylor and Jerry West. Over his career Wilt would break such diverse NBA records as field goal percentage, most rebounds in one game (43—against the Celtics, no less), and total assists in one game (21)—not to mention his stunning 100-point performance against the New York Knicks on March 2, 1962.

In short, the hapless Warriors blew it—big, big, *big* time.

The NFL Replay Misadventure

Entangled in a web of self-righteousness compounded by public outcries for abject fairness on the field, the NFL buckled to fan pressure invoking an instant replay folly that briefly changed the game, permanently tampered with the record books, altered how games are broadcast, and sparked a controversy that still smolders today. It deserves a significant ranking in the wake of its temporal grip on the history of pro football and a lingering, but wholly unnecessary controversy which denies any form of replay assistance to officials in any major sport.

Legions of fans and pundits, including the author, actually support the fundamental concept of instant replay. Many fail to see the problem in making use of available technology to reduce human error and render contests more consistent and fair, and ultimately to make the all-round game better. But for some reason the NFL injected more human error to contaminate the process, rendering instant replay nearly useless and, thus, *how* the NFL utilized replay became a major farce worthy of "blunder" consideration.

Although the NFL invoked the wrong use of replay in the first place— more on that below—even given the system adopted, the NFL ignored its own standards for reversing on-field calls. Officials were to be reversed only if video taped replays exposed "clear and convincing" evidence of an on-field error in the officials' decision. Yet those fans who remember instant replay well should recall numerous times when the replay officials in the booth also blew the call, and even more telling of the system's flaws were the painful moments of silence when those officials pondered on-field plays into near perpetuity, slowing down the game and telegraphing their own ignorance of the replay rules. If replay officials take several minutes to make up their minds, they are wrong by definition! How can a video taped error be *clear and convincing* if it takes forever to watch, analyze, review and second guess? This logic should have been patently obvious, especially to NFL league management, yet there seemed to have been no significant issue of it made in the press or otherwise at the time. The rule was excruciatingly simple: if it ain't obvious, don't change it! How hard is that? Yet the numskulls in the booth let their egos get away from them, feeding on self-indulgence and diluting the integrity of professional football proving, if nothing else, that the NFL blew its implementation of the replay system. Utilizing second-guessers in a booth upstairs provoked problems with improper training, intrusions of ego and power on the part of replay officials, tentative decision making on the field, television delays, and flat-out blown reversals.

The sensible way to employ instant replay is to make it available to the officials on the field to use when they see fit. Skeptical critics might argue that on-field refs would be reluctant to reverse themselves, but such concern is misplaced for two reasons: First, it is pure conjecture unsupported by reality. Why *would* the refs suddenly become so reluctant? If they blow a call, the whole world knows it whether the call is changed or not, so why not get it right and look good in the process? Besides, officials have a history of reversing themselves anyway, such as when one ref gets a better angle on a play and they all convene to talk it over and get it right. Second, if replay were implemented correctly by giving on-field officials discretion, then they would actually have to reverse themselves very seldom because they could examine questionable situations *before* making the call—they could always look first to examine whether the proverbial "foot was inbounds" or not.

Whatever the details of replay implementation might be, just *when* to use it should be discretionary, not mandatory; any other system of reviews and appeals is cumbersome, unworkable, and results in even less qualified people making calls—the second guessers in the booth. The reality of the situation will control the issue ninety percent of the time: if a coach goes ballistic on the sidelines, that always was and will continue to be a sign that something may be amiss, so the officials could react accordingly with more video information if they need it (sometimes they don't, if they had a clear view of the play), just as they do anyway when they talk over potentially wrong calls. Simply give the head official power to view replay on a sidelines monitor and trust him to convene the others to get it right when necessary. In fact, to add entertainment value to the process, let him—and the viewers—watch the same television footage at the same time. There is no need to add anything complicated to the system.

But if critics still are not satisfied, add one wrinkle to the equation: put one "quasi official" in the booth who would have no final review power, but who could signal the head official on the field to clue him in if television replay footage suggests a problem the on-field refs may be missing—but then let the referees deal with it as they see fit.

Instant replay should be implemented (and not just for football), but next time leave the skybox stooges out of it. If coaches insist, give them the right to ask for replay review by the head on-field official, but definitely charge the coach a time-out to minimize abuse and resultant game delays; otherwise, just make replay available to on-field "zebras" without sideline interference and let it go at that. Everyone would be happier, including the television audience, but more importantly the integrity of the game would be preserved without a convoluted system of trials, errors, appeals and second guessing.

CBS Loses NFL

On May 17, 1939, a nondescript experiment took place over a baseball game between Columbia and Princeton Universities: the game was shown on television. So far as we can gleen from the annals of broadcasting history, this was the first sports event ever televised in the United States. It did not play to good reviews, but it was the first in a stream of profound sports changes promulgated by television.

The NFL took root in the 1920's, but it did not begin to flourish until the 1950' when television began spreading pro football excitement to thousands, then millions of households. In 1951 the now defunct Dumont network televised five regular season games, plus the league championship, opening the door for a sports broadcasting explosion in the decades to come. By the mid-1950's, CBS began broadcasting certain NFL regular season games for $1.8 million per year, and NBC acquired the right to the NFL championship game. (Significantly, the broadcast rights in these early years belonged to the individual teams, not the league itself, setting the stage for other sports blunders involving the federal Sports Broadcasting Act and the NFL blackout rules.)

ABC began to aggressively pursue sports programming in 1959 (a move that would propel ABC from third place among networks in 1960 to the number one network overall by 1976) by cutting a deal with Gillette which promised ABC all its television advertising (beyond what was already contractually promised to NBC for the World Series) for a then staggering sum of $8.5 million.

In 1961 a combination of careful lobbying and well placed back scratching (see the Sports Broadcasting Act at blunder #20) Congress passed a law enabling the sports leagues, and in particular the NFL, to pool their television rights without illegally circumventing antitrust rules, allowing leagues to negotiate master TV deals for all the teams in one package. The first pooled rights contract was negotiated by CBS in 1961 with the NFL, establishing CBS as the preeminent network for pro football. CBS paid $4,650,000 to the NFL for each of the 1962 and 1963 seasons. In an ironic, foreboding precursor to quantum economic leaps to come, CBS outbid the other networks with an offer of $14.1 million for 1964.

The sports broadcasting explosion expanded until the early 1990's when CBS took a bath in sports programming—not in football, but on its four-year $1.08 billion baseball contract that expired in 1993. CBS finally caught a major sport in a downturn, as disgruntled viewers abandoned televised baseball, a phenomenon that would change the sports broadcasting landscape and eventually help launch the only successful new television broadcasting network in the modern electronic era: FOX Television.

With its fingers badly burned by Major League Baseball, CBS shunned the NFL by lowballing its contract offer and promptly lost its 38-year NFL relationship to upstart FOX's bid of $1.6 billion over four years, a "mere" $100 million per year more than the CBS ante. Without baseball or football, the once proud sports oriented network was left as an also-ran in a new market dominated by FOX, ABC and proliferating superstations and cable channels such as TNT, ESPN and now CNN/SI. CBS also lost icon sports announcers John Madden and Pat Summerall who defected, launching FOX and changing the sports viewing habits of America. It was all so unnecessary from the CBS standpoint, for the NFL was in full upswing, not Major League Baseball. By overpaying for Baseball, CBS forced itself to underbid the NFL, creating two huge mistakes out of one.

The Munich Basketball Team

There were many basketball teams at the Munich Olympics, of course, but the U.S. team stands out as embroiled in blunders, most of which were committed by the officials and unauthorized Olympic representatives.

Of course, in addition the U.S. team was still composed of amateurs only, part of an overall blunder covered elsewhere in this book; but most of all it was grotesque mismanagement at the game itself which gave the Russians a second and even third chance to win—illegally.

The U.S. team struggled through most of the game, a low scoring affair that could have used some great shooters, but rallied at the end to close within a point at 49-48. Doug Collins, big guard and pure shooter himself, then hustled to a loose ball and drove the basket drawing a foul with only three seconds left. Showcasing a competitive spirit that would later surface in the NBA with Philadelphia as a player and later in coaching both the Bulls and Pistons, Collins coolly sank two free throws to go up 50-49. The Russians inbounded the ball which was deflected as time apparently ran out; however, the Russians had called time out and play was stopped with one second showing on the clock. But for some reason the head of the International Amateur Basketball Federation (who was from Great Britain) jumped in at courtside and ordered two seconds back on the clock for a total of three. Not only was that absurd, essentially meaning that no time elapsed during the inbounds play, deflection, and then called time out, but it was outright illegal. Only the referees were empowered to make such decisions during a game, not an egotistical bureaucrat.

So then the Russians inbounded again, this time getting a shot off that missed, the horn sounded and crowds poured onto the court, the U.S. apparently winning the gold medal. But for some reason the clock had not properly registered the three seconds from before, so again the Great Britain bureaucrat and self-appointed control freak ordered the clock reset at three seconds, giving the Russians the ball for a third try with no time having elapsed. Then the referees directed the U.S. defender to back off the inbounds pass, which promptly was heaved the length of the court to 6'8" Aleksander Belov, who shoved back two American defenders as he scored at the buzzer for a 51-50 Russian win.

American basketball legend Hank Iba, who had coached previous teams to gold medals in 1964 and 1968, went ballistic, and had to be restrained when he went after the officials. Iba filed a protest, but that went nowhere since the appeals committee was controlled by three Soviet Block nations. All in all, the series of blunders added up to a Russian gold medal, not only changing Olympic history, but also contributing heavily to a grassroots call to open team eligibility up to U.S. professional players to counter the pros already employed by other countries, all of which led to the eventual "Dream Team" of U.S. stars in the 1980's and 1990's.

CHAPTER SIX:
Counting Down the Top 50...

The top fifty. As the stakes are raised, so go the sports blunders, sometimes exaggerated by sheer stupidity, often triggering significant changes in the world of sport as we know it. In the next ten examples, both the NCAA and SMU go amuck, a sports agent sets the legal standard for conflicts of interest, a gifted athlete dies in most dramatic fashion, sports television is changed forever, and Michael Jordan bails out unexpectedly. But first, the beginnings of the NFL:

The Staley Starchmakers

"Papa Bear" George Halas founded the Chicago Bears, the NFL, and just about everything of consequence concerning pro football.

He did not invent pro football, as a number of rag-tag teams popped up around the country from time to time, including one fielded by baseball owner Connie Mack, but he was the first to bring organization, vision and, most of all, respectability to a sport overshadowed by college football in the early modern era of Michigan, Notre Dame, Army, Navy, Harvard and Yale.

But football was not Halas' only passion. A rugged Chicagoan growing up in a Bohemian neighborhood, Halas set out for the University of Illinois in Champaign to play three different sports. Apparently preferring baseball, Halas eventually signed a pro contract with the New York Yankees, though his career there was nearly nonexistent. For about two weeks in 1919 he was the starting right fielder for the Yankees, even batting against the likes of legendary pitcher Walter Johnson who popped him up for an inauspicious out.

George Halas had a lifetime Major League batting average of .091 spanning a stellar career of twelve games. He was sent down to the minors, never to reappear.

Halas had played Big Ten halfback and end at the University of Illinois, so he resorted to football. But there wasn't much pro football in those days, so he landed in Decatur, Illinois (not far from Champaign) to play for a club team sponsored by Staley Starch Works, a huge grain, corn oil and starch processor. The Staley Starchmakers were not much of a team, but they paid fifty bucks a game. Showing a knack for marketing, if not showmanship, Halas took to promoting the team, drumming up fan interest in addition to playing football. He also beat some athletes out of the bushes, recruiting young men from college teams by promising them jobs at the Staley plant.

Halas next descended upon the owners of other factory backed teams, stumbling upon car dealer Ralph Hays who owned the Canton [Ohio] Bulldogs. (Note: The legacy car dealers as NFL owners apparently goes back nearly to day 1.) The Bulldogs happened to have a pretty good athlete, a guy who had a habit of winning Olympic events, by the name of Jim Thorpe. By September 17, 1920, Halas had finally assembled a meeting of eleven team owners to form a league of American Professional Football, later known as the National Football League. Each original franchise cost $100—they're worth close to $200 million now, not a bad return for the two original teams still in existence: the Bears themselves (from Decatur) and the Cardinals, then of Racine, Wisconsin.

The original league was a bit of a mess—sometimes one team would show up while the other, confused, was nowhere to be found—but that was not the blunder that lands the Staley Starchmakers on our list. It appears that Halas did too good of a job recruiting athletes and employees for Staley, and because company management began to feel overburdened with new salaries, the Staley owner just up and *gave* the team to Halas! This would be one of the biggest blunders in history, and save for the fact that no one could have foreseen the eventual folly of giving up the eventual Chicago Bears, not to mention the NFL itself, maybe it could have been the biggest overall.

Halas forged on with his new team, moving the struggling outcasts to a larger market: Chicago. A virtual one-man management team, Halas was ticket taker, owner, team captain and groundskeeper. In the early days Halas had a partner, co-player Dutch Sternaman, but Sternaman was bought out by entrepreneurial George in 1932 for $38,000—not a bad windfall for Sternaman since the U.S. was in the middle of the great depression—but it was still short-sighted enough perhaps to qualify as a blunder in its own right, especially since by this time the Bears were big news and had already signed legendary Red Grange—so if the Staley folly in granting the team to Halas were not enough, Sternaman's sell-out pushes it over the top, becoming the first of our top fifty greatest sports blunders of all time.

Shoeless Joe and the Hall of Fame

It is crucial for an organized sport—any sport—to maintain integrity. In the 1917 to 1927 period, Major League Baseball was rocked with scandals involving, by at least one published account, thirty-eight players. It was during this period that Baseball owners turned to a gruff, 38-year-old federal judge in Chicago, Kennesaw Mountain Landis, to take the helm as commissioner. Landis, who becomes a sports blunder in his own right later, had caught the attention of the owners when he presided over an earlier Baseball antitrust case. Displaying a combination of foresight and negotiating prowess, Landis convinced the owners to bestow sweeping powers upon the commissioner's office, so he is largely to blame for the fascist-like precedent that accompanied the office well into the 1990's.

Landis' first acts were to clean house but history observes him as somewhat of an enigma, for some accounts suggest he was too lenient while others are highly critical of his fascist-like approach to Baseball management. The most famous episode was the Chicago "Black Sox" scandal involving the 1919 World Series, but many other players bore the wrath of Landis. Many appear to have deserved it, such as the erstwhile Hal Chase, who was accused by his manager of trying to fix a game in 1910, later to be charged by manager Christy Mathewson of throwing games in 1917. He was also charged with bribery in 1918, suspended for throwing games in 1919, was alleged to have won $40,000 betting on the 1919 World Series, and was banned from the Pacific Coast League in 1920 for bribery.

Another player who was on the wrong end of Landis' ax-wielding power, Shoeless Joe Jackson, may not have been so deserving as Chase. By all statistical accounts, Shoeless Joe belongs in the Baseball Hall of Fame. Jackson batted over .370 four times in his career, including a sparkling .408 in 1911—only to finish second that year to Ty Cobb's .420. Shoeless Joe led the league in hits during both 1912 and 1913 with Cleveland, but hit "only" .338 in 1914 causing Cleveland to trade him to the Chicago White Sox during the 1915 season where he led the league in triples in 1916. In 1917 he hit .301 during the season and .304 in the World Series, as the White Sox defeated the Giants in six games.

By 1919, many White Sox players were at odds with owner Charles Comiskey over his penny-pinching salaries, but they still won the pennant with Joe Jackson hitting .351. They lost the Series to the Reds, however, which became the source of much finger pointing and trepidation. In 1920 Jackson was getting better, batting a stunning .382 for the season, leading the league again in triples. After the 1920 season, eight of the Sox players were indicted for throwing the Series, but in court they were acquitted of all charges. Even so, Landis banned all of them from Baseball for life, the effect of which was to "ignore" Shoeless Joe's hall of fame career, a Baseball campaign that rivaled other greats of the era such as Ty Cobb himself. (Cobb himself got into some questionable trouble regarding allegedly shady baseball dealing, but he was ultimately given a pass by Landis.)

History now largely suggests that Joe Jackson was innocent. Not only was he acquitted in court, his actual World Series performance had been nothing short of stellar, batting .375 for the Series and making many out-

110

standing defensive plays. And published sources concede it was likely he never received any money throughout the alleged ordeal.

The message sent in maintaining Jackson's ban from the Hall of Fame is a negative one, couched in a legacy of unfairness which should be reversed. It casts a pall over Baseball's storied past, creating a gaping hole in the Hall of Fame. It also lacks perspective, especially in comparison to the misdeeds of more contemporary players involved with drugs, mega-money and a variety of aberrant behavior. Baseball suffers a small erosion of credibility every time the Shoeless Joe issue surfaces, and it is a blunder to close its eyes and fail to rectify a wrong that has lasted more than a lifetime.

In addition to the impact upon Baseball, the banning of Shoeless Joe had to be a profound personal tragedy for Jackson who returned to his South Carolina home, operating a liquor store for the remainder of his days. Not much of a fate for one of the greatest ever to play the game.

The SMU Death Penalty

Much has been written about the powers of the NCAA, with considerable controversy over its fundamental fairness and investigative tactics. But sometimes one must beware of those who "protesteth too much," for intercollegiate athletics has endured more than its share of controversy and corruption. For example, one poll conducted in the mid-1980's by the *Washington Post* found that 82 college presidents admitted their respective institutions had been involved in athlete recruiting violations.

In June of 1985 NCAA representatives convened to enact a series of rules on cheating and related misconduct, one of which was the notorious "death penalty" which could be used to ban a sport entirely from universities that are frequent violators. At one time Tulane University actually killed its own basketball program in the wake of point shaving scandals, drug allegations and payoffs from pro gamblers.

But the symbolic number one award for such blunders goes to Southern Methodist University which achieved the most serious of all NCAA sanctions when its football program was nailed with the precedent setting "death penalty," an NCAA enforcement rule adopted in 1985, forcing SMU to give up its football program completely for three years.

This was an especially needless blunder on the part of SMU, for it had ample warning of rule violations in the program. It previously had to kick football boosters from riding the team plane, and later discovered that boosters had given at least one recruit $10,000 to sign with the program. Other players received cars and various amounts of cash, and when the illicit payments surfaced, the NCAA banned SMU from television. This was already the fifth time that SMU had been penalized since 1948, so when the program was finally killed for continued violations, it was no surprise to the NCAA and should not have been news to SMU, either.

47 O.J.

Somewhere in the top-50 it is fitting, although unfortunate, to address the O.J. Simpson debacle. Personal opinions of the author aside, the Simpson

murder trial episode was one blunder piled atop another, regardless of O.J.'s guilt. One jury found him the perpetrator of the now infamous slayings of his ex-wife Nicole and her friend Ron Goldman, and another found him "not guilty" of murder, though some of the jurors afterward hinted their verdicts were based more upon "reasonable doubt" proof problems, leaving open the fundamental question of whether he actually committed the gruesome acts. Without re-trying O.J. yet again in print, it is reason-

O.J.'s oddyssey: a rendezvous with destiny in the court of public opinion. (UPI/Corbis-Bettmann)

able to conclude O.J. was the likely killer based upon sum total of the two trials, subsequent expert opinions and literature, and reasonable inferences from photographic and forensic evidence, plus his failure to testify at the criminal trial (the latter fact being irrelevant in a court of law, but not in the court of public opinion).

Therefore, assuming O.J. was the perpetrator, it is appropriate to award a top-50 sports blunder even though he was long retired from a stellar college and pro football career. O.J. had been a concensus All-American at USC in 1967 and 1968, winning the Heisman Trophy in 1968 as well. Remarkably, Simpson played only 19 total games at USC, amassing an incredible 3,124 yards as a flashy running back for a 164 per-game average, amassing 33 touchdowns in the process. In the pros he was equally effective, leading the NFL with 1,251 yards in 1972, and becoming the first to rush for over 2,000 yards in an NFL season during the 1973 campaign. The rest, of course, is history.

In June of 1994 Simpson was charge with two of the most infamous murders in American history, and he went to trial on the criminal charges on January 23, 1995. Once again, the rest is history.

A case could be made that O.J.'s whole ordeal is not a "sports" blunder at all, which is why the events are placed in the middle of the pack and not higher. But they are worthy of overall consideration since O.J. was one of the greatest to ever play the game, and – retired or not – the tarnish on his career is inescapable. His Heisman Trophy is physically gone, and his sports marketing endorsements have gone up in smoke, adding a chill to the world of sports marketing, an industry already wary of athlete endorsers who can burn their sponsors with shocks and surprises from spouse abuse to drugs, arrests and other culpable indiscretions. And, assuming guilt, his actions are one of the most egregious mistakes ever made by a world class athlete.

16 Hank Gathers

Hank Gathers was a human being. He was also a nationally acclaimed basketball star at Loyola Marymount in California, a big game player and sure bet for the NBA.

Gathers represented the best and worst of American sports, but one should not be too hard on either, for it is a crime neither to provide a dream nor to follow one. But with the help of a few choice gaping holes in the system, Hank actually let himself down the worst way possible, committing a blunder of "top-50" proportions.

On December 9, 1989, Gathers was on the court in a Loyola-Marymount uniform, game in progress before a crowded gym of anxious onlookers. Hank Gathers shot a free throw and suddenly collapsed right there at the line, startling players and fans alike. Appearing to be unconscious, Gathers was whisked off via ambulance to the emergency room at Centinella Hospital. According to direct court documents from a subsequent lawsuit, Gathers was "visibly unconscious and underwent a tonic-clonic event and ... was noted to have an irregular heart rate by palpation by observers of the event."

But Gathers did not die from this incident. He remained in the hospital until December 11, 1989, undergoing batteries of tests during and after his stay. On December 18, 1989, Gathers was hospitalized again (this time at a different hospital) for more tests, and was diagnosed with irregular heartbeats, cardiac arrythmia. On December 20, 1989, Gathers was released from the hospital again, and one of his doctors wrote a release to Loyola Marymount stating, in part: "This letter should serve as the release for Mr. Eric Hank Gathers to return to full participation with the Loyola Marymount Basketball Team..." The letter went on to require the return be gradual, accompanied by continual heart monitoring.

The additional monitoring suggested an array of irregularities, so Gathers was placed on Proprananlol in prescribed dosages to help regulate and abolish "ventricular ectopic activity" (heart rhythm), a heart defibrillator was placed at courtside, and Gathers began to play competitively again. Some might suggest this return to the basketball court was his biggest blunder, but it was not.

Gathers' play was not up to par. It was sluggish and unproductive, at least in comparison to his prior superstar caliber. According to allegations in a subsequent wrongful death complaint, in January Gathers' coach (Paul Westhead) called his doctors to complain of the sluggish performance. The doctors conferred with Gathers and began reducing the dosage of his medicine. Also according to allegations later filed in court, Westhead again contacted the doctors and "urged that the medication be decreased." By Friday, March 2, 1990, the dosage had gradually been reduced from 240 to 40 milligrams per day as Gathers' on-court performance inched upward.

Just two days later, on March 4, 1990, at 5:14 pm, Hank Gathers again collapsed, this time while participating in a televised basketball game between Loyola Marymount and Portland before a live crowd of about 4,500 with many millions more watching on TV. Less than two hours later he was formally pronounced dead, and a subsequent autopsy pinned the cause of death on "idiopathic cardiomyopathy."

With that a star player—Hank had led the entire nation in both scoring and rebounding his junior year—and a young human being who deserved better, were gone.

Hindsight is dangerous. Nonetheless, a wrongful death lawsuit filed by Gathers' family on April 16, 1990, against Loyola Marymount, Paul Westhead and a host of medical personnel was settled for $2.6 million in 1992.

Even though he was an impressionable youngster who certainly was mishandled, to be fair to history and even to the late Gathers, his memory has to accept responsibility for the blunder: not because he wanted to play, not because he attempted to play with a disability (more on disabled athletes later), but because he was apparently a willing participant in manipulating his medication to improve sluggish performance. Staying on the full dose medication for a year would almost certainly have been the right choice. His blunder lay more with impatience than ambition, ignoring the truth rather than treating or working around the truth about his disability. In any event, his name has become synonymous with contemporary sports tragedies, and his dramatic death on television has burned a lasting image on sports history.

Foreman in Zaire

On October 30, 1974, Muhammad Ali did the impossible, defeating George Foreman to recapture the world heavyweight title. It was especially significant since Ali was in his fourth year since returning to the ring after a three-year layoff due to legal difficulties with the armed forces, and Ali was not in the same invincible condition he had once enjoyed. Foreman, on the other hand, was a behemoth, packing an almighty punch that invoked fear in all fighters, Ali included.

Foreman's ferocity even scared the media, with more than one reporter afraid for Ali's safety. Howard Cosell, who in effect grew up with Ali in the media, gave indications he even feared for Ali's life. Foreman had won the heavyweight gold medal for the U.S. at the 1968 Olympics, and he bashed Joe Frazier on January 22, 1973 to win the professional world title. Promoter extraordinaire Don King worked tirelessly to ink both Foreman and Ali in a blockbuster match, and so he found himself proposing a purse of $5 million each to induce the fighters into a contract. In need of monetary backing, King searched the world for deep pockets, finding them in the hands of strongman President Mobutu who staked the $10 million for a fight in Zaire, Africa.

In retrospect, perhaps Foreman's first blunder was to accept a fight in Africa, a land far removed by distance, politics and culture. George entered the country as an American, Ali as a black man, an advocate of human rights carrying the torch against the imperial legacy of slavery. Even though he was decidedly black, and certainly a gentleman, Foreman found himself in a hostile environment.

Some of Ali's people played upon Foreman's understandable paranoia under the circumstances, planting rumors that his food was being poisoned and causing George to switch hotels. Both fighters elected to train in Zaire for long periods before the fight, aggravating matters for Foreman in the intense heat and humidity, a negative factor for a large, heavy puncher with limited stamina in the first place. And then Foreman received a cut in training only days before the scheduled bout, which could hardly be deemed a blunder, but it was an aggravating circumstance that exacerbated the other blunders. One problem is that it delayed the fight, further isolating Foreman while Ali ate up the local culture and people, seemingly gaining strength from the delay.

Either Foreman failed to train properly or he underestimated the aging Ali—and maybe it was both—but either case was a blunder that factored into the fight and ultimate result. Published sources suggest Ali feared Foreman like he had no other, and he entered the fight with much trepidation. Foreman's punches lived up to expectations, thundering away at Ali. Muhammad relied on instinct and speed, but his eyes revealed profound concern even though he actually won the first round on points due mostly to quick footwork and a probing jab. In round two Ali shocked his entire entourage by getting caught on the ropes, Foreman blasting away with devastating blows. Ali's corner thought he had lost his mind and would surely be destroyed. But an unheralded quality of Ali was that he could take a punch and could overcome pain with the best of them.

This relentless punching kept up for three full rounds when, at the end of the fourth, Ali told his corner not to worry—Foreman the punching machine had finally worn out. "He's mine," proclaimed Ali, who nonetheless toyed with Foreman from rounds five through seven, with George getting more and more exhausted. Foreman, like Mike Tyson years later, was used to knocking opponents out in early rounds and his stamina was suspect. Eventually George ran completely out of gas, and as the eighth round wore on Ali let loose a barrage of five precise punches, knocking Foreman off his feet, onto the canvas and out for the count.

Ali had beaten the invincible Foreman by knockout, no doubt altering boxing history, not to mention Ali's. Muhammad would fight on, mostly winning but losing the title to Leon Spinks in 1978, only to win it back again seven months later before retiring and then returning for last hurrahs against Larry Holmes and Trevor Berbick—both losses.

Ludtke v. Kuhn

Baseball Commissioner Bowie Kuhn at one time must have been one of the most sued men in America. He was often taken to court by players such as Curt Flood, but he wasn't sued by sportswriters very often—until he met up with Melissa Ludtke in 1977.

Melissa was a writer for *Sports Illustrated* covering the World Series between the Yankees and Dodgers. Kuhn was an egotistical commissioner, bent on ruling Baseball and everything around it, including his edict against female sportswriters in the locker rooms. As fate would have it, the "irresistible force" of a determined Melissa Ludtke met the "immovable object" Kuhn when she attempted entry to the New York Yankees clubhouse.

Kuhn justified the exclusion of all women reporters for three reasons, first, to protect the privacy of the players, a misplaced concern since the players were ambivalent to receptive and because other means certainly could have been devised to protect privacy without excluding an entire class of people altogether. The other two reasons were not only less persuasive, they were insulting: 2) to protect the image of Baseball as a family sport, and 3) the preservation of traditional notions of decency and propriety.

Protect the image of Baseball as a family sport? Just what was Kuhn's vision of traditional decency—women are inferior, or naive, or tempting? Would a woman reporter convert Baseball into an "X" rated sex-fest? And who or what did he think was indecent—the reporter or the naked players? Nobody suggested Melissa was an indecent soul, and if it were the players why penalize her? If the situation itself were "indecent," why not regulate the situation rather than usurp equal protection from an entire class of professional female reporters?

The court agreed, issuing an injunction after clearing some technical Constitutional hurdles about state action, finding that Kuhn and the city-controlled Yankee Stadium had denied Ludtke equal protection under the Constitution of the United States. In a written opinion, the U.S. District

Court in New York disposed of Kuhn's first concern by balancing it unfavorably against the fundamental principles of due process and equal protection, and then addressed the remaining to points:

"The other two interests asserted by defendants, maintaining the status of baseball as a family sport and conforming to traditional notions of decency and propriety, are clearly too insubstantial to merit consideration."

Kuhn was blown out of the legal waters, and the face of professional sports reporting has never been the same.

Billy Sims v. Jerry Argovitz

Jerry Argovitz was a big time sports agent in the 1980's, representing high profile players including a number of notables in football. He also practically invented the standard of athlete-agent conflicts of interest.

In 1983 Argovitz was representing football superstar Billly Sims in his contract negotiations with the Detroit Lions. He also managed to land an ownership interest in a competing USFL franchise, the Houston Gamblers. Sims knew Argovitz had applied for the franchise, but he did not know the extent of his success or comprehend what it meant to him and Argovitz professionally.

Sims had been highly coveted in college, leading NCAA Division I schools with 1,762 yards and a 7.6 yard average. He also tied a record by rushing for over 200 yards in three consecutive games. After his senior years Sims was a first round draft choice of the Lions, gaining 1,303 yards in 313 carries and scoring 16 touchdowns in 1980.

Argovitz continued to negotiate with the Lions, and Detroit was moving in the right direction, wanting very much to retain Sims. Meanwhile, unbeknownst to Sims or the Lions, Argovitz began to throw roadblocks into the negotiations, and went to his own partner in the Gamblers to make Sims a competing offer to play in Houston. Argovitz embarked upon a scheme to wrestle Sims from the Lions by not returning calls, convincing Sims the

119

Lions were not interested, and then bringing Sims to Houston to meet with Argovitz's own partner on behalf of the Gamblers.

To the shock and dismay of the Detroit Lions, Sims eventually signed with Houston. A few months later, Argovitz presented Sims with a stack of papers to sign, one of which was a complete release and waiver of Argovitz's conflicts of interests and breaches of professional duties to Sims as his agent. Sims, understandably, did not have the benefit of independent advice through-out all of this, including the signing of these release papers.

When the Lions smelled a rat and Sims caught wind that something was amiss, the truth began to come out. The Lions joined Sims in suing Argovitz for conflict of interest, breach of fiduciary duty and rescission of contract. The court found the breaches "so egregious" that it threw out the Gamblers contract, freeing Sims to return to Detroit.

The Argovitz and Sims ordeal helped usher in a new era in American professional sports: the underbelly of sports representation, a sordid growth industry tarnishing the image of all agents, good and bad, and creating a free-for-all competition to sign big dollar athletes. Argovitz was not the first agent to be caught, and he certainly was not the last, but his blunder cost himself, the Lions, Sims and the USFL dearly.

The Heidi Game

On Sunday, November 17, 1968, the author was watching television, hardly an historic activity in itself, when the long awaited Raiders-Jets AFL football game was broadcast. The game was a marquee matchup between the scrappy Raiders sporting such luminaries as Daryle Lamonica and George Blanda against the then legendary New York Jets led by Broadway Joe Namath. Both teams were big draws for the American Football League in its heyday and later in the NFL, and both teams hated each other, adding to the suspense and coast-to-coast excitement.

The game did not disappoint, for it was a high scoring war resembling two heavyweights throwing endless punches until the bitter end, and with under two minutes to play, the game was tied at 29 each. The cagey Namath maneuvered his team into good field position, and at the 65-second mark teammate Jim Turner kicked a 26-yard field goal putting the Jets on top 32-29. True to form, NBC cut to a commercial, but when it ended the Jets and Raiders were nowhere in sight, supplanted by the Swiss Alps and Heidi the orphan girl herding her prized goats!

But there were still 65 seconds left in the game, a see-saw battle with two gutsy quarterbacks leading their vengeful teammates in a nationally telecast grudge war. While Heidi entertained a national sports audience tending her goats, Lamonica gunned a 20-yard pass, followed by a facemask penalty and a 43-yard touchdown pass with 42 seconds left for a 36-32 Raiders lead. On the ensuing kickoff, Jets return man Earl Christy muffed the ball at the 15 as it rolled through his legs. Although he retrieved it at the 10, the Raiders covered and hit Christy, spinning the ball loose. The Raiders recovered for a score, their second touchdown in nine seconds, neither of which was witnessed by the vast Heidi movie audience. The Jets took offense to the officiating and their assistant coach Joe Walton went ballistic, resulting in a number of fines from the commissioner. The author, and a few million others, saw none of the fireworks as we watched the dutiful Heidi.

NBC had allotted three hours for the game, which failed to cooperate by generating 19 penalties, chewing the clock up as 238 yards in total penalty yardage was walked off. It appeared to NBC that the Jets had won with about a minute left, so the network executives failed to interfere with the predetermined Heidi schedule, generating tens of thousands of complaints, hostile fans, and much egg for the faces of NBC management. The Heidi debacle, which was so needless and short-sighted given the Jets-Raiders rivalry, the known capabilities of quarterbacks Lamonica and Namath, and the vast national TV audience, would change the course of televised sports. It was the last time a major network planned to cut away a pro football game for prescheduled non-sports programming, symbolically elevating pro football to icon proportions as the NFL gradually supplanted Baseball as the national sport of choice.

Michael Jordan's Premature Retirement

One could write a book or a few lines about Michael's short-lived retirement in favor of minor league baseball, but the conclusion would be the same: it was a mistake. True to Michael's character, he was strong enough

to overcome pride and the mistake, returning not only to the sport he loves, but the sport he virtually owns like no other ever has and possibly never will.

Michael's own pride was capable of overcoming petty "I-told-you-so" concerns, and to his credit, he came back—and what a comeback it was. As rumors and hype of his impending return gained momentum, from March 7 to March 20, 1995, the stock of the major public companies he endorses went up in market value by a combined $3.8 billion! Cham-

Without MJ's sudden retirement, would the Bulls have won seven straight and counting? (Photo by Cindy Leo, UPI/Corbis-Bettmann)

pion Products added a third shift to fill 240,000 orders for the short-live but infamous #45 Jerseys, and the ratings for his first game back drew a 10.9 rating and 30 share—the highest totals ever for a regular season NBA game.

According to some published estimates, Michael's value to the league and local cities is something like $1 billion overall, and according to *Forbes Magazine* MJ personally raked in over $52 million in 1996 from earnings and endorsements without the effect of his $30+ million Bulls salary fully factored in. Forbes is on record suggesting MJ's total for 1997 could push $100 million, more than the annual gross revenues of a typical NBA team (at this writing about $90 million).

Batting .202 in the baseball minors only aggravated the sports blunder quotient of Michael's 17-month exodus, making it clear to everyone his departure was a mistake—certainly from a sports perspective if not a personal one. Clearly MJ's motives were influenced by his father's tragic death, heightened by the love he and his father had shared of baseball, making his whole retirement episode a human story just as much as a sports piece. But in the overall scheme of sports history, the import of the greatest pure basketball player in history suddenly checking out at the top of his game was a great misfortune to say the least. Had he not come back soon enough to salvage his career and even build upon his already lofty legend with two more championships (and counting) at the side of Scottie Pippen and, of all people, Dennis Rodman, MJ's prodigal behavior would rank much higher in the scheme of basketball and all of sports history. Luckily for him, the league and fans worldwide, it does not.

CHAPTER SEVEN:
Sweet Justice

As we crack the top third of blunders, courtrooms take on a greater presence with major cases influencing modern sports issues. No fewer than five of the next ten entries are lawsuits concerning free agency, disabled athletes, illiterate students, sex discrimination and the inimitable Jerry Tarkanian.

NHL Free Agency

Over time all major team sports have given in to varying forms of free agency, so to that extent the National Hockey League is not unique, but a major federal court decision rendered 1972 a watershed year for NHL players.

In the early 1970's the NHL maintained an especially oppressive reserve clause in its player contracts such that, in addition to restricting players from switching teams, the league also attempted to prevent players from leaving the league altogether. When the upstart World Hockey Association teams signed more than sixty NHL players, the NHL planned to block the mass exodus. The WHA countered with a federal antitrust action, attacking the restrictive nature of the reserve terms. The NHL argued that restrictions were necessary to preserve competitive balance, and that some restrictions would reasonably enjoy a valid business purpose.

Such an argument is not unique to professional sports, but the NHL registered a brutal loss on this one for two reasons: the restrictions, even against leaving the league altogether were too harsh; and the NHL intent was not just competitive balance within the league, but to snuff out all competitors. The was exposed by sports blunder #40 when Clarence Campbell, president of the NHL, explained on the record that the intent of the NHL was a determined drive to assure the NHL would always be "the only major professional hockey league operating from coast to coast in the United States or Canada."

The federal court enjoined the NHL from interfering, finding it violative of antitrust laws. The NHL may have lost anyway, but Mr. Campbell's expressed intent helped matters, and history, along.

Bulls and WGN vs. NBA

The explosive success of the National Basketball Association has perpetuated a long history of sports media wars as teams and the league fight for control over broadcasting rights to pro basketball games.

One such battle was waged in the trenches for years by the Chicago Bulls and Tribune-owned WGN Television against the NBA over superstation cable rights. NBA rules provided for league control of network broadcasts, allowing for a limited number of cable games to be controlled locally by teams and sold directly for superstation broadcasts. When the league sought to reduce the number of superstation games from 25 per season to 20, the Bulls and WGN brought suit alleging a Sherman Act conspiracy in restraint of trade. The U.S. District Court held for WGN in 1991 and was affirmed by the 7th U.S. Circuit Court of Appeals.

Often when litigation takes on marathon proportions, a blunder lurks behind the scenes on someone's part. Undaunted by its antitrust loss to WGN, the NBA pressed forward, citing new obstacles stemming from contractual commitments it made with the TNT cable station and implementing a "same night" rule that gave priority broadcast rights to TNT, which WGN found offensive, if not an outright antitrust violation. Again these titans marched to court, generating a series of decisions favoring WGN in

1992 and 1995 during a round robin of litigation over the applicability of the Sports Broadcasting Act (itself a top-20 blunder) and whether the NBA is subject to antitrust scrutiny. (The SBA was a work-of-art piece of federal legislation that gave permission for sports leagues to violate antitrust laws in pooling their television broadcast rights to be sold in packages to networks on behalf of the various teams.)

The WGN-Bulls-NBA war did not subside until December 12, 1996 when the two sides announced a settlement that leaves in place the number of local WGN Bulls telecasts at 35 (up from 20 during the course of the litigation) and allows for 15 Bulls games to be shown nationally on the WGN cable system each of the next two seasons, plus 12 more national games for the balance of the 1996-97 season. Although it was one of the latest in a chain of legal entanglements over the almighty broadcast dollar, it won't be the last—but it was a severe defeat to the NBA, one which tips relative revenues in favor of local teams rather than the league as a whole, especially where the popular Chicago Bulls are concerned.

Creighton University

In 1978 a hopeful young man named Kevin Ross enrolled at Creighton University, an established private university with a respectable cumulative student ACT of 23.2. Ross himself had scored only 9 out of a possible 36 on the ACT, but he was admitted anyway due to his 6'9" body and basketball prowess displayed as a high school star in Kansas City.

Ross was in way over his head, but he was fed courses like ceramics and theories of basketball to keep him eligible for the basketball team. After four years Ross had a cumulative "D" average, the reading skills of a seventh grader and overall language skill of a fourth grader.

Creighton helped Ross attend Chicago's Westside Preparatory School, a noteworthy school founded by the renowned Marva Collins. Ross attended for two years, then tried Roosevelt University in Chicago, dropping out almost immediately due to lack of funds.

Out of money and out of school, with his basketball career long behind him, Ross then fell apart. He exploded on July 23, 1987, when he was arrested for barricading himself in a Chicago high rise hotel and throwing hotel furniture onto the street. Not long after, he filed a federal lawsuit against Creighton alleging educational malpractice and breach of contract.

The sports blunder in question was more than just that, of course, it was a tragedy. The University was largely to blame, but so was Kevin Ross for getting himself into such a predicament in the first place. The overall system was culpable, too, for no safeguards saved Ross from his fate: none from the NCAA, the University or otherwise. In some ways the blunder had little direct impact upon the sports world, but it could also be argued its effect was profound and extensive, symbolizing the worst in American sports: letting down a young man who needed, even expected, much more. Most Americans have forgotten his name or the particulars of Ross' case, but many sports fans still refer to that "illiterate basketball player who graduated college," misstating the facts slightly, but aptly condemning the system's priorities, fueling the NCAA juggernaut and providing political fodder for years to come.

87 World Series Night Games

Major League Baseball has been struggling for at least a decade, maybe two. The cause cannot be attributed to one event, or even one class of events, but history does offer some insight.

There was a time when Baseball had so invaded the hearts of youngsters that they lived to hear fables of Mays, Mantle, and Drysdale—and before them Ted Williams and Babe Ruth—emulating their heroes at daily summer sandlot games. They not only traded baseball cards, they lived baseball cards, soaking up the stats like rays of sun and pining for those few elusive cards to round out the collection.

And they lived Major League games in their collective imagination through the miracle of radio, hanging on the colorful images of excitement as home runs rocked inner city stadiums in an age of afternoon baseball. Slowly the children drifted away, lured first by football and soccer, now basketball and video games. Baseball is not without blame. With monster salaries, big ticket prices, and less radio to exude the excitement of Major League ball, Baseball kept pushing the game into prime time and, as it happens, further away from America's youth.

Nothing symbolizes this more than the fate of the World Series. As the Series itself was lured by the night games of prime time television, youngsters were unable to keep up. The drama of Series games even as recently as the 1960's, which captivated the baby boom generation with day games and thrills, was suddenly less accessible to younger generations.

The Series itself has one of the most storied histories in all of sports, with endless legends, facts and lore. For example, pitching scoreless ball for the Red Sox in the 1916 Series was none other than Babe Ruth; game two of the 1922 Series was called due to darkness; the first consecutive sweeps in World Series history occurred in 1927 and 1928 as the mighty Yankees hammered the Pirates and Cardinals, respectively; Don Larsen pitched his perfect game in 1956; Dodger Sandy Koufax struck out a record 15 batters in the 1963 opener against the Yankees; and Bob Gibson struck out a record 17 Tigers in the 1968 opener.

Then something memorable happened: Bowie Kuhn became commissioner in 1969. Eager to lead Baseball into the promised land of money, Kuhn cut network television deals and, in the process, allowed himself and Baseball to bow to the demands of the electronic media by instituting night time—that is, prime time—World Series games, the first of which was launched in 1971. Was it the beginning of the end? Finding himself on a cold October night with falling temperatures as gametime approached, Kuhn stubbornly confronted the weather and his ego by steadfastly attending without a coat or hat so he would not appear cold to the television cameras, viewers, network executives and baseball purists. Thus Kuhn froze as Baseball was methodically burning, first disappearing and then self-destructing in the hearts of America's youth, many of whom to this day cannot see a late night World Series game to its conclusion. Such a shame. What a blunder.

Jerry Tarkanian vs. NCAA

The National Collegiate Athletic Association was originally organized to monitor safety in college football. Needless to say its jurisdiction has been expanded geometrically since its inception. Over 800 member institutions now comprise the NCAA, a private association governed by its own powerful executive committee.

One of the most compelling concerns of the NCAA today is amateurism, protecting schools, coaches and athletes from themselves by attempting to weed out gambling, under-the-table payments to players, and professional sports agents. From major point shaving scandals in the 1950's and 1940's to the corrupt influence of moneyed sports agents in the 1990's, the NCAA has had its work cut out.

But the end does not always justify the means, and the ominous enforcement powers of the NCAA are undergoing criticism, even attack, for running roughshod over due process, building cases on innuendo and hearsay with questionable regard for innocence. Innocent or guilty, one-time UNLV basketball coach Jerry Tarkanian was victimized by the unilateral power of an NCAA vendetta that led all the way to a United States Supreme Court decision in 1988.

"Tark the Shark" originally landed at the University of Nevada, Las Vegas, in 1973 after a successful stint at Long Beach State. A lackluster UNLV program needed a shot in the arm at the time, and Tark was it. By 1977 UNLV sported a lofty 29-3 record for the regular season and plunged deep into the NCAA tournament, making it to the exalted Final Four. In just five short seasons, UNLV's moribund program was at the NCAA pinnacle.

Success breeds many things, however, one of which is heightened scrutiny—especially when it comes too soon, or more importantly, is *perceived* to have arrived much too quickly. It could not have come at a worse time for Tarkanian, for the NCAA was already snooping around UNLV for alleged rule violations from before Tark's arrival, and Tarkanian's success, personality and tactics exacerbated an already tenuous situation. During the course of its investigation, the NCAA pinned additional violations on Tarkanian personally, and after the sparkling 1977 season forced UNLV to suspend him for two years for incidents allegedly involving payment for a flight home by one of the players, plus a shady grade changing episode. Tark had a hearing by the NCAA Infractions Committee, but it only consisted of NCAA investigator reports recounting hearsay stories they had heard, all balanced against contrary affidavits and documents presented by UNLV and Jerry Tarkanian. There was no oral testimony at all, let alone under oath, and as a result there was no cross examination of witnesses. In effect, Tarkanian was denied any right to confront witnesses against him, or even for adverse witnesses to appear and testify under oath. If that were not enough, he was also denied all right of appeal.

When the smoke cleared, UNLV believed it had no choice but to suspend Tarkanian at the direction of the NCAA. As an employee of the University, Tarkanian was actually a public employee of the state, and at the time it is interesting to note he was Nevada's *highest paid* public employee—a distinction that says much about the importance of sports in society.

Tarkanian sued both UNLV and the NCAA, and by the time the U.S. Supreme Court took the case, the UNLV basketball program was a huge success with great notoriety. The central legal issue became one of "state action," summarized this way: The government cannot legally abridge due process or equal protection, but save for a few specific statutory exceptions private organizations have few restrictions. This case was significant because there were two very different defendants in UNLV, clearly a state actor, and the NCAA, a wholly private association. Complicating matters, the private NCAA found itself giving directives to the public UNLV, so who was controlling what?

The Tark argued that the NCAA had become so intertwined with UNLV that the distinction was blurred, if not erased altogether. Tarkanian was probably right on all points of his legal arguments; that is, state action is what denied him due process, and secondarily the state had never proven a case against him and his program. But Tarkanian had a huge impediment to overcome: himself. The quick successes of UNLV were legendary and suspicious. The players had a habit of turning up in the wrong company, the NCAA allegations were clearly viewed in the "where there's smoke there's fire" context, and much of the country—including many justices on the Supreme Court—was aware that the importance of sports and winning had become grossly distorted. With all of these factors, it was politically difficult for Tarkanian to win. Sometimes bad facts can create bad law, and that is exactly what happened.

True to form, five of the nine Supreme Court justices voted against Tarkanian, determining the NCAA-UNLV duo was not a state actor. To their great credit, however, four justices exposed this legal fiction for what it was, an aberration. Justices White, Brennan, Marshall and O'Connor wrote a dissenting opinion upholding the lower Nevada courts which had already found for Tarkanian. But they were not enough, falling just one vote short of a 5-4 majority, allowing bad law to stand and effectively unleashing an already overzealous NCAA upon athletes and universities for at least the next decade.

Wright v. Columbia University

Disabilities are one of the last frontiers of "acceptable" discrimination. Why? We are a society obsessed with interfering with peoples' lives "for their own good." Although these attitudes still invade the workplace, fostering discrimination against persons who can do their jobs in spite of their disabilities, nowhere is it more prevalent than the world of sports.

We applaud major league pitcher Jim Abbott who performed in spite of having only one hand, but during his whole life he must have fought the naysayers who insisted he couldn't play baseball, that it would be too unsafe, that he couldn't field the ball and protect himself, or that he might fly out of control and hit a batter while off balance. There are many who would have kept him out of baseball "for his own good," such as doctors, coaches, parents, school board members—you name it.

Can a football player play with one kidney? Can another play with only one eye? High school star running back John Wright, blind in one eye since birth, believed he could play college football. He enrolled at Columbia University, only for the school to block him from its varsity football team due to his handicap. True to himself, Wright filed a federal lawsuit citing a violation by Columbia of the Federal Rehabilitation Act of 1973, which makes it unlawful for any institution receiving federal funds to discriminate against disabled individuals.

In essence, the Rehab Act states that no one can be denied an opportunity on the basis of a handicap if such person can perform in spite of his or her disability. However, there are at least three nuances, indeed exceptions, to the rule. Applied to athletics, the first qualification is that the fundamental sport must remain unchanged. For example, a wheelchair basketball player will be denied the opportunity to play Big Ten varsity basketball even if he has a wicked outside shot because having one wheelchair player on the court changes the fundamentals of the game. Second, one must not present a material risk to others and, third, there must not be a likelihood of substantial harm to the disabled athlete. Using the same wheelchair example, the athlete himself may not be at material risk, but the awkward presence of the wheelchair in a fast paced game could pose a material threat of harm to the other players.

Was John Wright the one-eyed football player a material risk to other athletes? Probably not. Did his condition cause a likelihood of substantial harm to himself? Columbia University argued it did. Wright countered with experts who testified that no substantial risk of serious eye injury exists as a result of playing football. The school, in effect, hid behind the "for your own good" argument, a cause that at one time partially kept Black Americans on the back of the bus "for their own good," or kept girls out of interschool sports for the same reason.

But federal law now says there must be more than a simple incremental increase in risk to oneself, for we all have the fundamental right to make our own choices. The court listened to plaintiff's experts, and also found Wright himself mature enough to appreciate and weigh the risks involved as he was a mature individual with a "B" average and a host of high school academic and athletic awards. Wright won his case in 1981, setting a precedent for many disabled athletes to follow years later. Major athletic programs are full of otherwise disabled players, including those with diabetes, heart conditions, missing limbs, missing eyes, asthma, AIDS, and many others.

It is difficult to understand the motives of Columbia, which stood only to deny a young man's dream perhaps for fear of being sued or just because it had a jealous compulsion for control. If it was to avoid litigation, it failed miserably, losing one of the leading landmark disability decisions for athletes under the Rehab Act of 1973.

Jabbar from Milwaukee to L.A.

Lewis Ferdinand Alcindor, Jr., began life in 1947 in New York, New York, starting an historical journey that would end with a new faith and name, Kareem Abdul-Jabbar, and with the most points scored in NBA history: 38,387. His point totals are far ahead of number two Wilt Chamberlain, and Jabbar is so far beyond Michael Jordan that MJ would have to maintain a torrid scoring pace for up to six more years after 1996-97 to catch up (another reason Jordan's ill-fated retirement warrants the blunder list).

Known primarily for his marquee play as a Laker, many fans forget Jabbar was a three-time MVP while still with Milwaukee, his first NBA home fresh out of UCLA (where he was Lew Alcindor, changing his name after the 1968 season). He was NBA rookie of the year in 1969-70, scoring 2,361 points with 1,190 rebounds. He was also the first-team NBA all-star center as a Milwaukee Buck in 1971, 1972, 1973 and 1974. In effect, Jabbar had an entire all-star career just in Milwaukee, already winning the NBA championship (1970-71) and more key awards than most players in a lifetime.

As a collegian at UCLA, Alcindor won the NCAA championship three consecutive years, averaging over 26 points per game for his entire college career. At 7'2" and 235 pounds, Jabbar was quick, strong and mobile—catching the eye of every pro scout and general manager. Since he could do everything from pass to score to rebound to shot blocking, Jabbar has been compared to a *combined* package of Chamberlain and Russell. He was also cunning, smart and patient, deadly traits for a competitor with a prototype physical package.

So what did Milwaukee do in 1975? They traded him—to the L.A. Lakers—and neither team has been the same since. After an all-star career in Milwaukee, Jabbar continued for 14 more seasons, winning five additional NBA championships as a Laker and setting a host of nearly unbeatable personal records. Milwaukee has struggled, fielding teams over the years from good to bad to indifferent, but never again threatening to win the championship.

Bad trades happen regularly, of course, and they are often easy to second guess—but trading a proven icon even before reaching his peak was a blunder, pure and simple.

Cohen v. Brown University

The gender revolution in sports is becoming an overnight success 10,000 years in the making. It was gradually taking shape in the last half century, but progress was initially very slow before Congress enacted federal Title IX legislation in 1972, literally making it illegal to discriminate against female athletes, and others, in education.

On April 21, 1997, the movement received a colossal boost from the U.S. Supreme Court, promulgated by a now notorious blunder by Brown University. The Court refused to hear further appeals by the university, letting stand lower decisions for plaintiff Cohen, formerly a student at Brown in 1991 when the university announced a plan to reduce its overall athletic budget by cutting out two varsity sports including two women's teams (volleyball and gymnastics) and two men's teams (water polo and golf). According to court records, Brown savings attributable to the cuts were approximately $61,000 annually for the women's teams and $16,000 for the men, impacting 37 men and 23 women student-athletes. Brown students in all four sports still had the option of playing on respective club teams without university funding. Even so, a federal district court agreed with Cohen and enjoined the cuts, finding them violative of Title IX, the key language of which is quite succinct:

No person in the United States shall, on the basis of sex, be excluded from participation in, be denied the benefits of, or be subjected to discrimination under any education program or activity receiving Federal financial assistance.

There are statutory exceptions, of course, but these are far from controversial: educational institutions of religious organizations with contrary religious tenets; social fraternities and sororities; father-son and mother-daughter activities at educational institutions; scholarship awards for beauty pageant winners; and a few others.

When Brown University elected to implement its athletic cuts, it plunged into an abyss of litigation which lasted about six years, all over just $76,000 of budget issues—and in the end, after losing at every court level, Brown submitted to the courts its own Title IX compliance plan calling for:

*Expansion of women's opportunities within the existing program, but without adding teams in sports not currently offered;

*Establishing and enforcing minimum roster sizes for all teams;

*Establishing and enforcing firm limits on the roster sizes of all men's teams;

*Implementation of a formula for determining the target number of male athletes that would result in absolute rather than substantial mirroring.

The University probably could have avoided protracted litigation, considerable effort, some dubious press, and a not-so-friendly posture toward women's athletics had it implemented a reasonable compliance plan under court supervision, but instead it forged ahead with no apparent material gain at stake. Although there has been no shortage of Title IX cases concerning athletic programs, the post-1992 decisions clearly reflect the Brown court influence vindicating the plaintiff Cohen and her female classmates. In this regard, Brown University has done much for Title IX clarification and progress, but clearly at its own expense in the annals of sports history, though not in the manner originally intended.

32 Scottie Pippen's Contract

This is a personal favorite of the author, for it takes a relatively small blunder and projects it into a meaningful glitch of NBA history.

Bulls star Scottie Pippen signed an eight-year, $21 million playing contract with the Bulls which, barring trade possibilities, assured his Bulls career through the 1997-98 season. When Scottie originally inked the deal, it must have looked good—maybe for about a year or so. But it wasn't long before contracts of lesser players doubled his, and then salaries shot well over the $50-million mark with Big Dog Glenn Robinson and others. It is now dwarfed by Shaq's $100 million and Michael Jordan's $30+ million per year, and even dwarfed by journeymen role players commanding $6 million to $10 million a season like, for example, his oddball teammate Dennis Rodman.

But had Scottie Pippen signed a short-term deal, which as a rising superstar in a league full of exploding salaries he should have done, he never would have remained a Bull. After a couple of championships, or at least after the Bulls' third championship and Michael's retirement when Scottie became the laboring oar for the team, it is likely Scottie would have both demanded and commanded huge dollars—sums he would have gotten from other teams with deep pockets and even deeper ambition such as the Knicks, Lakers, Sonics or others. And had Scottie bolted early, the likelihood of all those Bulls championships diminishes and maybe even Jordan's own mystique suffers without Scottie's presence on the floor.

The only constants in all the Bulls championships have been MJ, Scottie and coach Phil Jackson. All the other role players have come and gone from John Paxson (gone) to Bill Cartwright (gone) to B.J. Armstrong (gone) to Horace Grant (gone) and many others. Scottie's contract actually helped in two ways. First, it kept him on the floor in Chicago and, second, it did wonders for the Bulls salary cap and related fiscal planning. Without Pippen's low salary, the Bulls may not have been able to purchase the right mercenaries to perpetuate the championship runs. If Scottie were at $10 million a year now, along with MJ's $30 million, where would the rest of the team be? The whole 1997 normal team salary cap was around $27 million. Bulls fans have reaped considerable reward, much of it at Scottie's unfortunate expense.

The Retirement of Bobby Jones

Golf is a sport that thrives upon blunders, but virtually all of them seem to occur on the tee, in the water, in the sand, on the adjacent fairway—all playing blunders which do not technically qualify for our sports blunders "100." And golfers seem to be a stable lot as a group, making mistakes here and there but not really turning the sport upside down.

But history may give us one mistake in hindsight that is useful to both honor golf and highlight one of its greatest stars, Bobby Jones. Not many whippersnappers under the age of 60 remember Jones, this author included, but we've heard his name and have an occasional vague appreciation for his legacy, even if all golfers are not entirely sure of what it was.

For starters, over one eight-year stretch Bobby Jones won the U.S. Amateur title five times, the U.S. Open four times, the British Open three, and the British Amateur once. Jones won the U.S. Open for the first time in 1923, and won it for the last time in 1930. And in between he didn't do too poorly: over each of those eight years Jones either won the Open outright or finished in a tie for first, necessitating a playoff. He tried the British Open four times altogether, winning three of them. He also took the Grand Slam in 1930—winning everything in sight.

Was an unbeatable Bobby Jones the "Michael Jordan" of golf?
(UPI/Corbis-Bettmann)

Jones was one of the first great protégés, predating Tiger Woods by the better part of a century. Jones began playing at age five and officially broke 80 when he was 12. He won the Georgia amateur championship at age 14, and seven years later he had scored his first victory in the U.S. Open.

To this day when the galleries line up for the Masters at Augusta, they traverse the great golf course created by Bobby Jones himself, playing in the tournament co-founded by Jones in his native Georgia in 1934. The Jones of his era was nearly unbeatable, much like Michael Jordan of today—though with less national fanfare. Like Jordan, though, Jones was inspired to retire early, suddenly dropping out in 1930 at age 28, clearly on top of his game—and it was one of the greatest games of all time. History may never know all of Jones' motives (he said he had simply played enough under the rigors of tournament demands), just as we may never really understand or appreciated MJ's own short-lived retirement, but it surely was a mistake to snuff out his own career which could have set standards for greatness that no one could have even considered breaking.

Along the way Jones graduated from Georgia Tech and even Harvard Law School, though he never practiced law. And even though he retired in 1930, Jones played in his own Masters Tournament for fun from 1934 to 1947 when he withdrew due to a shoulder difficulty which later manifested itself as the initial stages of a more severe spinal problem which eventually confined the great champion to a wheelchair, perhaps exacerbating the loss suffered to himself and all of golf by virtue of his early retirement.

CHAPTER EIGHT:
But That Was The Rule *Yesterday...*

The countdown gets interesting with rule changes, more lawsuits and four Baseball blunders. The NFL is well represented, also, with its anti-corporate ownership rule, its lawsuit with Cowboys owner Jerry Jones, and the old Rozelle Rule which played havoc with player freedom, later going down in flames and taking NFL free agency control with it.

NFL Corporate Ownership Rule

For some reason NFL owners have maintained a bias against corporate ownership—probably a euphemism for big money owners—long after it makes sense even in the context of their own self interest.

Excepting the unique municipal ownership of the Green Bay Packers, the NFL has mostly shunned the corporate ownership concept while other leagues have embraced it (Disney and the Mighty Ducks; the Chicago Cubs and the Tribune Companies; and the publicly held Boston Celtics). At one time such concept may have been necessary to preserve the mom and pop owners whose roots went back to the inception of the NFL (the George Halas family, for example), but with modern salary caps the concern over big money spenders is largely misplaced.

Potential conflicts over the rule have not always been mere speculation, for in the early 1990's the NFL nearly lost a monstrous antitrust case to the

141

Sullivan family, former owners of the New England Patriots. In the late 1980's Patriots owner Billy Sullivan wanted to take the team public, selling off 49% in a public offering similar to the Celtics, who had just sold off 40% of the team in a public offering at the end of 1986. (The family needed money, it appears, primarily due to his son's less than successful foray into the world of promoting national rock concerts.) NFL rules precluded such an offering, so Sullivan eventually sold to entrepreneur Victor Kiam in 1988 for $84 million. When Kiam sold the team again in 1992 at $110 million and a healthy profit, Sullivan believed his family had been illegally denied full value for the team and the flexibility of public ownership, prompting an antitrust suit against the NFL.

Sullivan actually went to trial and won the case, gaining $17 million in damages, trebled to $51 million per antitrust guidelines law, losing it all later in a marathon litigation war that found a court of appeals sympathetic to his overall case but finding that earlier league votes on the issue and other technicalities precluded his recovery.

The NFL anti-corporate ownership rules actually depress team values and, in the salary cap era, they are unnecessary if the motive is to keep player compensation under control.

The Rozelle Rule

Sandwiched between the era of NFL free agency and its one-time early stranglehold on player freedom was a hybrid period when the NFL pretended to embrace free agency with a device quickly labeled the Rozelle Rule after the league's namesake commissioner.

In the 1960's and 1970's, the NFL operated under a reserve system that automatically tied players to their teams for two years, after which they could switch teams by playing one more year under their old contract, subject to a ten percent pay cut, a procedure known as "playing out one's option." If a player did switch teams before 1963 (which rarely happened), then the new team could sign him without owing any compensation to the former club. In 1963 the rules were changed, requiring the two teams to either agree upon compensation or, if they could not, then the commissioner would take over consistent with the following excerpt from the newly adopted by-laws:

> "...the Commissioner may name and then award to the former club one or more players, from the Active, Reserve, or Selection List (including future selection choices) of the acquiring club as the Commissioner in his sole discretion deems fair and equitable; any such decision by the Commissioner shall be final and conclusive."

This was the essence of the Rozelle Rule, and its practical effect was to severely chill player movement. From 1963 through 1974 a total of 176 players played out their options. Only about 20% of them actually signed with new teams, and in 30 out of 34 cases the clubs either waived or agreed upon compensation. So in eleven years, only four times did a player actually change teams without the agreement of the clubs, causing Rozelle to invoke the compensation rule.

This is how it worked until the now legendary player John Mackey stood up and challenged the rule as an antitrust violation. In 1976 the United States Court of Appeals agreed, finding the Rozelle Rule to be an unreasonable restraint of trade. The NFL had argued that the rule was necessary to maintain competitive balance and to protect club investments in scouting and player development. But the court was unimpressed for three reasons. First, the rule applied to all players of all ability levels, not just the superstars; second, it was unlimited, enabling teams to tie up players for their whole careers; and, third, the rule had no procedural safeguards, thus enabling the commissioner to "wing" it. Rozelle himself could be gracious, punitive, fair, or hostile without restraint or any clue as to what he might do. The rule also proclaimed such power "final and conclusive," so an aggrieved player had no right of appeal. Therefore, since the clubs were working together through Rozelle to perpetuate the rule, such conduct was in effect a conspiracy to restrain trade that had no legally redeeming value. Sometimes restraints can be justified if they serve to enhance competition, not just squelch it, which is why the draft, an obvious conspiracy, is allowed—it is deemed necessary to achieve a certain minimum competitive balance to keep all the clubs, and the league itself, in business.

But the Rozelle rule was draconian in nature, giving Rozelle the discretion to follow any whim—including the ability to be unreasonable, arbitrary or punitive. The NFL's steadfast, greedy adherence to the rule in the face of changing economic and legal times was a blunder, leading to a spectacular courtroom loss in the Mackey case, opening the floodgates to NFL free agency.

28. Hill vs. NCAA

Curtailing improper drug use is a noble objective. Sometimes it is even crucial, such as drug testing of airline pilots and other workers where safety for others is paramount.

But drug testing is suspect not for its laudable objectives, but for who does the testing of *whom*—and why. *Hill vs. NCAA* was a 1994 California Supreme Court case that analyzed and endorsed a new, stringent NCAA drug testing program for college athletes. Critics, including one justice who contributed a strong dissent to the court's opinion, express concern that the NCAA did not distinguish between performance enhancing drugs, illegal recreational drugs such as marijuana, and necessary prescription drugs. The concern extended to an apparent discrimination against student-athletes as opposed to other students in general.

The regulation of performance enhancing drugs in athletics is legitimate, logical, and wholly necessary to make the system work. Without regulation, all athletes would soon be required to take as many drugs as possible to keep up, reducing legitimate sports competition to a drug dare fiasco. However, without endorsing marijuana for anyone, consider how far the NCAA has gone: even though marijuana has no performance enhancing qualities, college athletes are subjected to random tests, full disclosure to strangers about their entire medical history, providing blood for testing, and being required to urinate in the presence of drug monitors—all of which are serious invasions of privacy, if not just plain humiliating. But other students do not go through such rigors—not students in the music department, engineering, history, economics or drama. These people can drive cars, go to class or skip class, take marijuana or not, and never have to give blood or urine for the privilege of studying music, architecture or business.

In the very first year of the NCAA drug testing program in 1986-87, the precise time when drug use should logically be the most prevalent, less than one percent of tested NCAA athletes were declared ineligible due to drug use of any kind. And of those suspended, 75% were football players on steroids. The issue is not the banning of performance enhancing drugs, the issue is whether to suspend the Constitution for citizens who happen to pursue athletics in college. The issue may not be so clear for pro athletes, although privacy considerations still remain, but at least the pros are paid huge sums for the privilege of competing. They can afford lawyers, they have unions to look after them and help fight the system where necessary. College students, though, are very much disadvantaged in fighting the system one on one. And there is no compelling reason to invade their privacy on a random basis, especially to test for anything and everything that might be in their systems—even when all their fellow students are allowed full, unabridged freedom. Sometimes the cure is worse than the disease, and this is the essence of the NCAA blunder and of all those who blindly condone its arbitrary power. Consider it this way: when someone has possession and control of your blood and urine to test for steroids, it is tempting to test for everything, to snoop into one's system essentially, and there is no reason to believe the NCAA drug and medical voyeurs have any concerns for privacy and decency, let alone the Constitution. If any large group in America should be randomly tested for illicit substances, it should be drivers of automobiles— or at least convicted drunk drivers who are one of the greatest menaces to life in America today—but any suggestion that their rights to drive and to privacy be curtailed brings a Constitutional posse out of the woodwork every time. Until society gets its priorities straight, it is hard to endorse a private sector of power-happy drug enforcers hiding behind the red herring

NCAA concerns over whether a student-athlete has taken too many sleeping pills, allergy pills or even marijuana. If we test them, why not all students everywhere? And if all students are tested, why not all automobile drivers? But why stop there? Let's just test everybody in America—the question is, who are we going to empower to do the testing, keeping in mind the old, but dauntingly true adage that "power corrupts"?

Selig the Commissioner

Major League Baseball in the 1990's became a leaky boat with no rudder. Fan and network television interest is waning and licensed merchandise sales, once on top in the sports marketing world, are falling far behind both the NFL and NBA. Without a permanent, independent commissioner, Baseball doomed itself to a lack of direction without objective leadership, rendering Baseball vulnerable to criticism, failure and possible legal attacks targeting its arbitrary management and growing internal conflicts of interest.

Perhaps as an overreaction to its last powerful commissioner in the form of Bowie Kuhn, who even turned his near-boundless power against the owners themselves, Baseball ownership elected to coast with one of their own at the helm: acting commissioner Alan "Bud" Selig. Kuhn was commissioner of Major League Baseball during a watershed period of great change, jealously wielding his power with ruthless abandon and, consequently, was one of the most sued men in America, defending himself and Baseball against the likes of star player Curt Flood and innovative owners Charlie Finley and Ted Turner.

Since the appointment of Judge Kennesaw Mountain Landis after the 1919 Black Sox World Series scandal, Major League Baseball has operated with independent commissioners (if you could call Landis independent), albeit some stronger or more bull-headed than others—that is, until Bud Selig. As owner of the Milwaukee Brewers franchise, acting commissioner Selig was by definition not independent, having an inescapable bias regarding the players and, possibly, against particular other owners. The potential conflicts were so egregious that his every act attracts scrutiny, especially if the commissioner's mandates reek of vacillation and doubt. Case in point: Roberto Alomar.

At the end of the 1996 regular season, Orioles star Alomar spit in the face of umpire John Hirschbeck. Was Alomar suspended without pay as NBA star Dennis Rodman has been so many times before? Did he receive a hefty fine *a la* the Bears' Bryan Cox who flashed an obscene gesture to an NFL official, for which he was assessed an $87,500 penalty? With the Baltimore Orioles poised for a playoff run and Major League Baseball still suffering a backlash of apathy following the cancellation of the 1994 World Series, Selig suspended Roberto Alomar for only five games *with* pay. Not only did Alomar receive the equivalent of a week's paid vacation, Selig compounded the brutally obvious pandering of Alomar and the Orioles by skipping the 1996 playoffs and delaying the suspension until the harmless beginning of the 1997 regular season. The umpires were so enraged by such a weak-kneed approach they threatened a labor action. Although Baseball narrowly escaped a potentially crippling walk-out by umpires, the umps announced a "zero tolerance" plan for on-field antics beginning the 1997 season.

Contrasted to the Alomar incident, when White Sox journeyman Tony Phillips forayed into the stands to seek out and eventually punch a fan, his volatile act was met with all the force of a limp mop when he received a measly $5,000 fine and no suspension, smacking of a big legal no-no: arbitrary sanctions. From the standpoint of legal theory and common sense, the next transgressor who commits an offense no more serious than either Alomar or Phillips will cry foul if his penalty is out of line, boxing the commissioner into a peculiar range of silly fines and non-suspensions.

If Baseball were to retain a non-independent commissioner, it would forever walk an indelible tightrope spanning a sea of potential bias and resultant player-management-umpire-fan hostility. Pete Rose, caught in a web of gambling entanglements, nearly beat commissioner Giamatti on a bias theory; Bowie Kuhn narrowly escaped the wrath of Charlie Finley who sued Kuhn for arbitrary behavior when he vetoed the sale of three of Finley's Oakland ball players; rogue Braves owner Ted Turner did score a partial victory when Kuhn intervened in Turner's acquisition of Giants star Gary Matthews; and then Kuhn did lose outright to Melissa Ludtke, the *Sports Illustrated* writer who was unconstitutionally banned from the Yankees clubhouse. Even the independent commissioners had trouble demonstrating fairness, so imagine the potential donnybrook if a truly biased commissioner were thrown into the fray. Independent commissioners are the norm for all leagues in today's big time sports environment, and by putting Bud Selig in the middle the owners diluted their credibility and exposed Selig, themselves and all of Baseball to potential criticism, liability—and more.

Jabbar's Lost Fortunes

This is a quirky entry in the blunder list. It is one of those "but for" events that seem insignificant on the surface, but have long-term profound effects.

In the 1970's and 1980's, one Thomas Collins was a super successful sports agent specializing in big name basketball players such as Ralph Sampson, Terry Cummings and Kareem Abdul-Jabbar. By the late 1980's, though, Collins was on the wrong end of a lawsuit by Jabbar, who alleged large losses of funds due to failure to prepare and file tax returns, comingling of funds, converting funds and debts, and flushing Jabbar's fortunes into ill-fated real estate deals. These transgressions had great significance for Jabbar, of course, but they also affected pro basketball in a most abstruse way: many of the NBA all-time career records got warped. How?

It was widely reported and believed that Jabbar played at least two extra years in the NBA because of his personal financial difficulties. Assuming that to be largely true, it not only directly impacted a number of NBA records, it propelled many of them out of reach. Not only did Jabbar become the all-time scoring leader (more on that shortly), he set all kinds of diverse records such as most defensive rebounds (even ahead of Chamber-

Kareem Abdul-Jabbar's (seen here keeping an eye on team mate Magic Johnson) off-court problems could have contributed to on-court records that may never be broken. (Photo by Alan Zanger, UPI/Corbis-Bettmann)

lain and Russell), most personal fouls, most minutes played (10,000 minutes more than Wilt), most seasons of 1,000 or more points (19), most career field goals made and most field goals attempted and most blocked shots.

Now for the big one: Kareem Abdul-Jabbar scored 38,387 total career points, almost 7,000 more points than the unstoppable Wilt Chamberlain who occupies second place on the all-time list. Based upon his occasional pointed comments in the press, it is logical to believe Bulls star Michael Jordan has Chamberlain's level in his sights, a realistic goal over the next two seasons at this writing. But catching Jabbar might be impossible, for Jordan would then have to essentially lead the league in scoring (around 30 points per game) for three *more* straight years, even after catching Chamberlain, to surpass 38,387, all of which means MJ would have to maintain his current level of full-time play for about five more years altogether until around age 40 or so. Given MJ's determination, one should not fully discount the possibilities, but if he tries, the domino effect of Jabbar's lost fortunes will continue to influence basketball, extending Jordan's career as he chases records and rainbows—all due to the indiscretions of a now forgotten sports agent and the pride filled determination of one Kareem Abdul-Jabbar.

NFL vs. Jerry Jones

Sports marketing has become nearly as big as the sports themselves. From television ads to athlete endorsements, events management to licensing, the marketing side of sports is a multibillion-dollar industry.

Most licensing is league and team oriented, such as the licensing and sale of logos on sweatshirts, hats and T-shirts, and big money is at stake. In fiscal 1996 the NFL sold the most licensed merchandise of any league: $3.4 billion. The NFL take on gross sales is in the eight to nine percent range, so rounding it off the NFL may have realized close to $300 million in license fees for 1996 alone, approaching about $10 million per team. The NBA is second at $3.1 billion gross, Major League Baseball third ($1.5 billion), with the NHL fourth ($1.0 billion).

The leagues are aggressive marketers, and these relative sales levels are by no means static. Baseball has been collapsing, dropping 6% from 1995 to 1996, following even bigger prior drops due to the strike, cancellation of the World Series in 1994 and waning fan interest. Baseball, which used to be a strong #1 is now entrenched at #3 not far ahead of hockey. The NBA is charging forward, but it showed signs of vulnerability when Michael Jordan retired and sales went flat. But the NFL appears to be on top for awhile, for its one year sales gain in 1996 was the greatest of all the major pro leagues at +8%.

A new phenomenon is now emerging: the private deal. Michael Jordan is already a one-man endorsement machine all his own, and Cowboys owner Jerry Jones discovered a loophole around NFL licensing rules by cutting outside sponsors into his stadium deals. In August of 1995, Jones teamed up with Pepsi in what was reported as "the financial shot heard round the NFL," completing a package where Pepsi would pay $40 million to Jones' empire for exclusive right to peddle soft drinks at Texas Stadium for ten years. This was a financial declaration of war against the NFL, which had already charged Coke $250 million for a 5-year stadium deal within the league as a whole. NFL Commissioner Paul Tagliabue publicly called Jones "shortsighted and self-serving," probably using even stronger adjectives in private. San Francisco owner Eddie DeBartolo was less diplomatic, accusing Jones in the press of "being like a heroin addict" presumably in his quest for money.

NFL member clubs have a league agreement, and they have a long history of cooperation in such matters as the draft, free agency, drug testing and product licensing. Just how far the NFL reach can legally extend will be for the courts to decide, as the NFL sued Jones for violating the NFL agreement. But even that may not resolve the issue, for what about Pepsi? Pepsi might then sue the NFL for an antitrust violation, the league agreement being a restrain of trade.

Either way, someone has committed a blunder here, probably the NFL for sitting on a loophole in its league agreement with the owners, potentially putting millions, if not billions, of sports dollars up for grabs.

The 1963 Strike Zone

Baseball with its long history has evolved through many eras of dead balls, lively balls, speed, power, pitching and platooning. When the 1960's emerged, speed was beginning to factor into team offenses, a philosophy bolstered by baserunning specialist Maury Wills who stole a headline record 104 bases in 1962. As offensive production picked up, the Baseball rules committee believed the pitchers needed help—just why fewer runs was more desirable is still a mystery—so they voted to enlarge the strike zone to include the area from a batter's shoulders to the bottom of his knees, as opposed to the armpits to the top of the knees.

This little maneuver, taken without approval of the clubs themselves, sent Baseball offenses into a tailspin. With high strikes and low strikes in their arsenal, pitchers gunned down batters without mercy, creating another "era of the pitcher" with such 1960's stars as Koufax, Drysdale, Gibson,

Marichal, McNally and many others—topped off by Denny McLain's 31 victories in 1968. Home run output in 1963 dropped by 10% and total runs by 12% to only 3.9 per game.

At the same time, many teams also were moving into new ball parks which were normally more roomy with vast foul territory and cavernous outfields. By the end of the 1960's, the pitchers were dominating baseball, turning games into soccer matches with lots of defense and very little scoring, perhaps triggering the beginning of the end for fan enthusiasm and blind support.

Dropping the Pitcher's Mound—1969

The 1963 blunder of expanding the strike zone created so much havoc in favor of pitchers that by 1969 the baseball rules committee was desperate to reverse the error. Not only did they reinstate the old strike zone (from the armpits to the top of the knee), but they dropped the height of the pitcher's mound and invoked strict enforcement procedures in monitoring the mound size.

Baseball offense exploded, once again producing .350 hitters and 40 home run seasons during the 1970's, a decade of resurgence for Baseball, including George Foster's 52 homers in 1977, Willie Stargell's 296 dingers during the decade, and both a Reds team (in 1975) and an Orioles team (1970) that won 108 games in one season. Rod Carew hit .388 in 1977, batting .343 for the whole ten years. Extended fan interest was also evidenced by a plethora of baseball books between 1969 and 1975 such as Jim Bouton's *Ball Four*; *The Boys of Summer*; *The Summer Game*; Philip Roth's *The Great American Novel*; *Babe*; and the infamous *Nice Guys Finish Last* by Leo Durocher. Baseball heroes were monster hitters again: Carlton Fisk, George Foster, Willie Stargell, Reggie Jackson.

Baseball was back—for awhile—but it need not and would not have left in the first place, but for the strike zone antics in 1963. The tinkering in both 1969 and 1963 is worth two blunders since one beget the other, and since the 1969 rules changes not only brought back the old strike zone but also lowered the pitcher's mound—setting the rollercoaster stage for 1970's and 1980's baseball before its virtual collapse during the 1990's.

ABA-NBA Merger Fiasco

In the world of sports economics, nothing works like competition. Before the American Basketball Association was launched the median salary of an NBA player was $23,000 per year, and after its inception in 1966 the NBA median jumped by almost 100% to $43,000.

The storied history of the NBA traces its roots, of course, to the invention of basketball by Dr. James A. Naismith in 1892. Five years later Yale found itself beating Penn in the first five-on-five game of intercollegiate basketball ever, and later a barnstorming team was organized in 1914 as the New York Celtics which, after World War I, became the first pro basketball team on record. An association of teams called the National Basketball League was assembled in 1937, after which various other competing leagues were attempted, and in 1949 two of the early leagues merged to become today's NBA.

Encouraged by fan interest and occasional television exposure, the NBA began to prosper during the 1950's and 1960's. A new competing league was formed in 1961 by the owner of the Harlem Globetrotters, but it failed to take hold, going out of business only two years later. But in 1966 the American Basketball Association was launched, and it took root, cutting into the NBA turf. Players were jumping leagues, sports agents proliferated, lawsuits were filed—it was like the old west revisited with gunslinging lawyers behind every gym.

When the ABA and NBA began merger talks, they were actually sued by NBA star Oscar Robertson at the behest of the NBA Players Association, alleging antitrust violations and hoping to maintain the wide open competition of the two leagues which was driving salaries straight up. The NBA was ill prepared and began losing in court, forcing a massive settlement in 1976 which governed player-league relationships for ten years. The NBA lost its perpetual option clause, and teams could only retain the rights to sign a drafted player for one year, after which he returned to the following draft class. If a player could hang on for two years without signing, the new rules allowed him to become a free agent.

The owners struggled with these new parameters until 1983, when they finally bought peace with the players by implementing a salary cap system and allocating 53% of gross NBA income to the players—an innovative but extremely expensive price. This was the foundation for the key NBA cap and compensation rules today which govern, even define, the contemporary NBA which had let the compensation "cat" out of the bag as it backpedaled out of the Robertson lawsuit.

Kennesaw Mountain Landis

Landis caught the attention of major league owners as the federal trial judge who oversaw the landmark Federal Baseball League antitrust suit, the decision that was the basis for the U.S. Supreme Court decision that found Baseball was not a business engaged in interstate commerce (see Blunder #1). The owners liked his style and pegged him as commissioner to oversee a sport rife with corruption, not the least of which was the 1919 Black Sox scandal. It is tempting to call Landis a hero, not a blunder, for he cleaned house, wrested power away from the owners and probably saved Major League Baseball. But the owners allowed Landis to anoint himself God of Baseball, the all-powerful commissioner whose "best interests of Baseball" powers allowed him to run roughshod over players, owners and even the game itself. Sure, the nasty, power hungry Landis managed to save Baseball, but that doesn't mean a more cerebral, forward thinker could not have done the same without destroying careers in the process.

The era of Baseball scandal, which ended more or less in 1927, saw 38 major league players embroiled in controversy. In addition to the eight Black Sox players banned by Baseball, eleven other major leaguers were also thrown out. Rumor has it that Ty Cobb was about to be banned, too, but stardom, politics and some well-placed back scratching probably saved him. And those Black Sox players were actually acquitted in a court of law, but Landis threw them out anyway—just *because* he could—coldly destroying one of the greatest players in the history of the game, Shoeless Joe Jackson, who history generally exonerates from the scandal because of his outstanding World Series performance.

But even Landis' power-mad assault on gambling, the players and even the owners was not his worst contribution to Baseball. Landis governed with an iron will of prejudice, keeping Baseball Lilly white all the way to his grave. Kennesaw Mountain Landis died in 1944, and it was immediately thereafter in 1945 that Branch Rickey embraced and first signed African American Jackie Robinson with the blessing of new commissioner Happy Chandler, breaking the historic racial barriers of Major League Baseball.

CHAPTER NINE:
The NFL Takes On...

As we delve into the top-20, the NFL takes historical shape, losing out to the fledgling AFL but nimbly defeating competition from the upstart United State Football League, and successfully lobbying for the federal Sports Broadcasting Act to beef up its television monopoly powers. Boxing rises to the fore also, with two mishaps by the one and only Muhammad Ali.

Sports Broadcasting Act

In 1961 Congress buckled under pressure from Pete Rozelle and the NFL by enacting the federal Sports Broadcasting Act exempting the leagues from antitrust restrictions in the pooled sale of television broadcast rights.

This was probably a blunder, which is nothing new for national politics, since it bestowed legal monopoly powers for the leagues to negotiate television deals en masse, activities that would have otherwise been illegal without the protection of Congress. By definition it also gave them the power to choose what games to televise, not to mention how and when, a significant development since few factors over the last 30 years have influenced modern sports more than television and its tidal wave of money, money and more money.

Money begs controversy, though, and after Rozelle's Congressional lobbying in the early 1960's the courts became clogged with battles over media dollars and control of the airwaves. It all began in 1939 with a small experiment during the Columbia and Princeton baseball game on May 17: it was shown on television. The electronic media would have little influence over sports for the following decade, but as television flourished in the 1950's, an adolescent National Football League began to capture America under the leadership of George "Papa Bear" Halas, the founder of the Chicago Bears and the NFL itself.

In 1951 the now defunct Dumont Network televised five regular season NFL games, plus the league championship, opening the door for an explosion in sports broadcasting. By the mid-'50's, CBS began broadcasting certain designated regular season games, paying a total of $1.8 million per year. ABC aggressively pursued sports programming in 1959 when it cut a deal with Gillette to offer televised sports for a then staggering sum of $8.5 million. Throughout this period, the teams were free to make their own television deals, which they did with sporadic success. Enter the youthful but perceptive NFL commissioner Pete Rozelle who believed the league's competitiveness eventually would be jeopardized if teams in major television markets continued to sell their respective broadcast rights individually. Under Rozelle's leadership in 1961, the NFL teams agreed to sell their collective television rights as a single package and share broadcast revenues equally among all franchises.

With the Sports Broadcasting Act firmly in place, NFL revenues began to accelerate in the early 1960's. CBS paid the league $4.65 million for each of the 1962 and 1963 seasons. In 1964 CBS outbid the other networks with an offer of $14 million, and in that same year the fledgling American Football League struck a five-year deal with NBC for $36 million. Ten years later the three networks collectively anted up $186 million just for football, and by 1982 the total football spending had exploded to $2.1 billion—500 times what it was just 20 years earlier.

Even so, Rozelle and Congress were still not through. By the mid-1960's the NFL and competing AFL finally punched each other out in bidding wars over everyone from Joe Namath to John Brodie, so league merger plans were born. Fearing antitrust roadblocks to the proposed merger, the two leagues looked to Congress when they consummated a merger agreement in 1966. If Congress were to amend the Act by allowing the league merger, even though such had nothing directly to do with television, the league would expand into New Orleans, home of powerful committee chairs from Louisiana, Sen. Russell long and Rep. Hale Boggs. In short order a bizarre amendment to the Sports Broadcasting Act was tacked on, allowing league mergers in the face of antitrust laws, and the new franchise was awarded: the New Orleans Saints.

Tyson vs. Holyfield

It seems as though Mike Tyson's professional life has been one long chain blunder with one mishap leading to another. With reported fight earnings of over $100 million since Tyson's return from the last fateful blunder, his Indianapolis rape conviction, Tyson not only bit off a part of champion Evander Holyfield's right ear, he may have ripped the heart out of his own career. As the once invincible Tyson presses into his thirties, he can ill afford another layoff from boxing, yet he must endure a lifetime Nevada suspension that will likely be honored by all state boxing commissions, potentially bringing his ring career to a screeching halt.

Because of his parole from the rape conviction, Tyson cannot even leave the country to fight lucrative matches overseas, now piling one blunder on top of another. The gravity of his rape and subsequent conviction was greater by itself, but the biting incident ranks higher due to its sheer stupidity on the heels of all that has transpired and the severity of the current blows to his fighting career. It will also do more to influence professional boxing on the whole, with regulators now getting more into the act, all the while Tyson left a lasting impression of disgust on the general public, if not boxing authorities worldwide.

Tyson may apply for the return of his license in one year, and if he fails he may try again once per year thereafter. If he changes his attitude plus personal and professional image significantly, the license could possibly be reinstated, but all the years he will have missed will never be recaptured. It is therefore difficult to avoid the obvious analogy: the person most adept at knocking Tyson out for the count has been, of all people, Tyson himself.

Walters and Bloom

If anyone could be credited with inventing the sports agent business, it probably would be Mark McCormack, founder of the Cleveland-based International Management Group. McCormack originally hooked up with golf superstar Arnold Palmer, penetrating the golf business by matching players with endorsements and other marketing ventures.

With the sports business about to explode, IMG's timing was faultless. Its performance wasn't bad, either; first it swooped up golfers and tennis players, and then penetrated team sports such as football. With total revenues in the estimated range of $1 billion annually, IMG is a monolith in the sports representation and marketing business, but it is by no means the only kid on the block.

As new agents sprung up, the industry was slow to regulate the representation business, giving it a "wild west" shoot-out image, somewhat superficially portrayed by Hollywood's *Jerry Maguire*. The industry has been rife with fast talkers and charlatan agents, but the two who took the underbelly of the sports agent business to new lows were Norby Walters and Lloyd Bloom, who not only engaged in illicit payoffs of prospect college athletes, they relied upon them, first paying off and then signing estimates of 50 to 60 players. One player, former Auburn star Brent Fullwood, who was picked fourth overall in the 1987 NFL draft by the Green Bay Packers, was sued by Walters and Bloom when Fullwood fired them and refused to pay back $4,000 in under-the-table money. Both the payoffs and the agency representation agreement were violations of NCAA rules, and although the court was less than sympathetic to either side, it refused to enforce the "loan" repayment, expressly refusing to act as "paymaster of the wages of crime or referee between thieves," dismissing the case against Fullwood.

But Walters and Bloom were not through. As it happens they took their payoffs seriously, even threatening to break the legs of others players who attempted to extricate themselves from the Walters and Bloom grip, catching the attention of federal prosecutors. Both were indicted and convicted of mail fraud in a Chicago federal court, a decision that was later overturned on appeal for technical reasons. Bloom, although a young man, died shortly thereafter, and Walters was discredited as a legitimate sports agent. Their meteoric rise and dramatic fall from grace is one of the most volatile turnarounds in sports, and the high profile of their descent led to a restructuring of laws, state regulation and NCAA scrutiny which largely defines the sports agent business today.

The NBA Lottery

All the major professional sports leagues in America conduct an annual draft of new talent, and for the most part such a draft has withstood antitrust challenges as a necessary "evil" to assure parity and the long-term financial viability of the respective leagues. But for many years the NBA has conducted its draft of incoming rookies like no other: the worst team does not necessarily pick first.

In the 1980's the NBA perceived criticism about league games at the end of each season, specifically whether any of the poor teams would deliberately lose games to get a shot at the off-season number one pick. This is an issue that seems to surface only in basketball, as opposed to hockey, football or baseball, and may even be a false issue at that.

It doesn't even come up in baseball probably because there are very few rookie impact players. Major Leaguers don't just show up at the doorstep, they are groomed in the minor leagues, and stars are almost impossible to pick, with many outstanding players coming after the 20th and even 40th rounds. To throw even one baseball game for a shot at the number 1 pick in almost every case would be a foolhardy crap shoot, and hockey has similar attributes with its strong farm system and a host of minor leagues. Only on occasion has the NFL been criticized for such a ploy, but it was never taken very seriously, at least not to the point of shaking up the rules to accommodate alleged concerns. Therefore, like always, the team with the worst NFL record still gets the number one pick, and so on up the ladder.

The NBA, on the other hand, has modified the system such that the bottom six clubs enter a random lottery to see who picks first, second, and so on. This is supposed to eliminate the incentive to lose, but does it work? It sounds good on the surface, but the scheme has a telltale twist: weighting the teams with bad records so they have a greater chance for the first pick, or at least one of the top two or three selections. But now aren't we back where we started, with the team with the worst record having a decided advantage over the other teams, even those in the lottery pick formula?

Consider also the sheer logic, or lack thereof, behind the lottery program. If any influence over team attitude is attained, maybe it is just shifted from the bottom team to the club seventh from the bottom, which now has to wrestle the lure of a lottery pick. The NBA would argue that the weighting system counters this issue, and it may be right, but it is this same weighting system that gives back the incentive of bottom teams to stay at or as near the bottom as possible.

And none of this hyperbole addresses the central question in the first place: were NBA teams intentionally losing games to get the first pick? Certainly the NBA hasn't said they were for sure, and on the surface it is difficult to tell for if they were losing games at the end of the season, it could have been because they were bad teams—which is why they were in the standings basement to begin with.

So with all that, the NBA lottery has become a media circus, with television soaking up the random drama of selecting the draft order of bottom teams. It even takes on a game-show atmosphere, with team representatives lined up in front of the cameras like contestants. As the draft sequence unfolds, team logos are placed on a board and the cameras zoom in on the elation or dejection of the club reps. Basically the NBA lottery is just television, a staged event as part of the great NBA marketing circus—and overall not a bad circus it is, since the NBA is one of the best run leagues around. But the lottery system is a mistake, an outright blunder, for it suggests the NBA cannot control team behavior at the end of a given season, and then it creates a fictional process by which top draft picks are randomly shuffled all over the bottom of the league, changing NBA history forever. For example, the 1986-87 Clippers could have, and probably should have, picked future NBA star David Robinson with the first pick—but the lottery got in the way as it does every year until perhaps one day the fairness issue will surface and the NBA drops the lottery charade.

16 The Jimmy Carter Boycott

The consensus of American history seems to assess President Carter a better human being than a president—and maybe that's not all bad—but regardless of his standing among political pundits, Carter made a sports blunder of top-20 proportions when he led the American boycott of the 1980 Olympic Games.

Carter's objectives were noble, and if world politics outranks world sports, maybe his choice was right. But on balance it was a monster sports blunder, and here's why:

In 1979 the Soviet Union brazenly invaded Afghanistan, committing human rights violations of world proportions. The western world cried out for a harsh statement in protest, and Carter selected a boycott of the 1980 Olympics. This was a blunder already, for the Olympic ideal is for all nations, regardless of politics and international strife, to drop enough hostility for two-plus weeks every four years in a symbol of joint humanity, showing to the world and themselves that civilization has the power to recognize the ideals of peace and human cooperation in spite of any and all differences, even if the harmony is just temporary.

Why Carter chose the Olympics is for historians to muse, for the reasons are most certainly complex rather than simplistic (maybe it was better than war; or maybe Carter was just too ineffective to bluff the threat of war and needed a venue he could control—who knows), but having pulled the United States out of the 1980 Olympics Carter destroyed the dreams of many young athletes, robbed Americans and much of the world of a chance to share in the Olympic ideals, pulled the rug out from under not only sports fans but most Americans who look forward to the high drama of the greatest of all international sports events, and set a precedent for other countries to use and misuse the Olympics as a forum for world demagoguery—which is exactly what the Russians did.

The 1984 Olympics in Los Angeles set the stage for Soviet retaliation, and they went for it, boycotting America's Olympics just four years after Carter's original fiasco. Thus, not one Olympics was shattered, but two. Not until 1988 did the Games return to some semblance of normalcy, a full twelve years after the last untampered Games in 1976.

Spencer Haywood vs. NBA

Spencer Haywood was a star basketball player in college, on the U.S. Olympic team, in the old ABA and then the NBA. He also is one of the reasons the ABA succeeded as a competitor to the NBA, later merging to comprise a formidable combined league, *and* Haywood is the chief reason the NBA must not exclude college underclassmen and even high school seniors from its draft process.

Bad as NCAA rules are now, they used to be worse, and when sophomore Spencer Haywood became disgruntled with NCAA rules that allowed him to earn only fifteen dollars per month for laundry money, he bolted college. Because of NBA rules, he couldn't go there, for in an attempt to appease its college counterparts, the NBA banned underclassmen from its own draft. That was probably sub-blunder #1, for Haywood had no legitimate place to go except the competing ABA which had no firm exclusionary rule. This allowed the ABA to pirate talent that otherwise would have been available, shrinking the NBA base of great players and putting the ABA on the map.

Haywood then signed with the ABA Denver Rockets, but played there only one year before attempting to renegotiate his deal, causing the Rockets to sue his agents for interference of contract. While the case was still pending, Haywood then signed with the NBA Supersonics and when the NBA made noises about intervening, Haywood sued them, too, challenging the validity of the four-year rule imposed upon college players eligible for the NBA draft.

If inducing Haywood to sue it was not NBA sub-blunder #2, then losing the case was. A federal judge in California ruled the NBA rule on college players was an antitrust violation, illegally excluding a class of players from draft consideration. So the NBA exclusionary rules on eligibility induced a series of legal and contractual mishaps that shaped the character of the league today, even to the point of signing players as high school graduates, sometimes with no college background at all.

14 Ali and the Armed Forces

On April 28, 1967, Muhammad Ali refused induction into the armed forces. Perhaps no one but Ali will ever know the precise reasons, but although he clearly wanted no part of the Vietnam War, it is unlikely he was a simple draft dodger. Had Ali been inducted, he probably could have received special boxing assignments or other singular treatment to keep him from the front lines. On the other hand, perhaps Ali did not trust what was then a white establishment in the military, especially given his perceived militant status and public connection to the Black Muslims.

If we take him at his word, Ali's refusal was the product of his religious beliefs. It is difficult to doubt him, not only by reason of his apparent passion, but because the alternatives are illogical. A stint in the services would have been finite (two years), but failure to be inducted carried a five-year prison term, not to mention the loss of his boxing title and career—no small matters to risk unless, perhaps, his religious (and political?) beliefs were genuine.

Even so, from a sports perspective Ali's action was a blunder. From the standpoint of history, maybe it wasn't a blunder at all; maybe it was heroic—after all, many endeavors appear foolhardy on the surface only to yield profound greatness later (i.e., Columbus, Bell, and the Wright brothers). Ali's stand no doubt contributes to his popularity today, for public attitude about the war shifted to, as they say, Ali's corner. In 1967 the public was largely behind the war, or at least it still supported the government and the draft, so Ali's refusal was not wholly popular, especially with middle America.

Stripping Ali's Title

If Ali's refusal to be inducted was one blunder, stripping his title was worse. Since when in America did one have to pass a political and religious beliefs test to be a champion? In view of today's antics, from the destructive (Mike Tyson) to the negative (Albert Belle) to the benign distraction (Dennis Rodman), Ali's actions and beliefs seem tame, if not laudable. The contrast with Mike Tyson's many misadventures is tempting, for Tyson's rape conviction kept him out of action for roughly the same time that Ali missed. (For the record, three and a half years elapsed from Ali's refusal of induction until his next fight against Jerry Quarry on October 26, 1970.)

Ali was prosecuted under federal law for failing to report when drafted and was convicted during a two-day jury trial in June of 1967. He was sentenced to five years in prison, but remained out on bail during the course of his appeals. In the meantime, while the criminal appellate process was running its course, Ali sued the New York State Athletic Commission, the body that had revoked his championship. The Commission had suspended his license on April 28, 1967, the exact day he refused induction. This was before his criminal trial, so the Commission had convicted him even before the courts did—and without a hearing at that, although the Commission said it would grant a later hearing after the criminal trial was completed. For some reason Ali's lawyers failed to request the hearing until two years later, and when the Commission then refused, Ali brought suit. Ali lost his suit for procedural reasons, and he lost every other court battle, too, save for the most important one: the Supreme Court of the United States eventually overturned his conviction, which triggered a reversal of the Athletic Commission action in suspending his license, reopening the door for Ali's boxing career. Discouraged, Ali had actually announced his retirement on February 3, 1970, but found himself in the ring again just eight months later, defeating Jerry Quarry in a three-round TKO.

The "Greatest" took on all comers from the Olympics to the federal government, Foreman to Frazier, but his stubborn will may have been both his greatest strength and worst enemy. (UPI/Corbis-Bettmann)

Ali went on to fight Joe Frazier to regain the World Heavyweight title on March 8, 1971, but he narrowly lost a 15-round decision. Ali became a very active fighter with three more bouts in 1971, six fights in 1972, and four more in 1973. The following year would be one of the greatest of Ali's career. On January 28, 1974, Ali defeated Frazier in a rematch, but he did not win back the World title, because Frazier had already lost it—to a monster power punching behemoth in the form of George Foreman. On October 30, 1974, with the whole world watching, Ali challenged the imposing Foreman in Zaire, improvising a fight plan that took advantage of the heat and humidity as Foreman punched himself out of gas. A flurry by Ali in the eighth round caught Foreman off guard and unable to defend, giving Ali an historic knockout to finally regain the title he had lost over *seven years* before!

Ali continued to defend his championship, winning ten straight title bouts over the course of 1975, 1976 and 1977. When he defeated Earnie Shavers on September 29, 1977, more than ten long years had elapsed since he lost his title to, for all practical purposes, the federal government.

12 USFL vs. NFL

Perhaps inspired by the success of the American Football League (see Blunder #11), the United States Football League was founded in May of 1982, beginning league play almost a year later in March, 1983. The USFL intentionally placed teams in major television markets (Chicago, Boston, L.A., New Jersey, Philadelphia, etc.) and succeeded in luring television contracts with ESPN and ABC. The USFL also elected to play a spring schedule, avoiding head-to-head competition with the NFL.

The new league was initially cost conscious and established budget guidelines for player salaries at around $1.5 million per team. It wasn't exactly a salary cap, but it revealed league wariness of bidding wars for players. The USFL seemed to embark on the right foot, garnering an $18 million commitment from ABC over two years, plus $11 million from ESPN during the same time period. It was still David vs. Goliath, though, for the NFL television deals included a $2.1 billion contract over five years from 1982 to 1986.

Notwithstanding its desire for constraint, the league nevertheless signed star Herschel Walker to a three-year deal for $3,250,000 gaining significant media exposure in the process. In the first week of play, TV ratings were comparable to the NFL, but they dwindled after that. On the whole, the league lost $40 million its first year—about fifty percent greater than projections. The USFL commissioner pleaded for salary caps to save the league from itself, but it fell upon deaf ears. Soon after, the L.A. team committed $40 million to Brigham Young quarterback Steve Young and the spending spree was on. Then some owners pressed to switch league play to the fall, forcing a head-to-head confrontation with the NFL, mostly to force a merger of some teams into the NFL.

As the league struggled television retained its interest, with ABC exercising a renewal option and anteing up $175 million over four years beginning in 1986, and ESPN offering a three-year $70 million package. The USFL then voted to move league play—and television coverage, of course—to the fall for 1986. This move went beyond a blunder, it was economic suicide. According to court records stemming from an eventual antitrust lawsuit by the USFL against the NFL, the fall switch was made notwithstanding clear warnings of failure: (a) ABC warned that such a move would breach its television contract; (b) the move was contrary to the recommendations of the USFL's own independent management consulting firm; and (c) the USFL internal marketing and operations people were against it.

After the announcement of the planned fall move, USFL interest nose-dived while ratings plummeted. In October of 1984, the USFL played its "Trump" card, suing the NFL to appease some of its owners who wanted to force a merger, including the high profile owner of the New Jersey Generals, Donald Trump. The 1986 season never got off the ground, and if it had there was only one team left in a top-ten TV market: New Jersey. Over a three-year period USFL teams had abandoned 14 of the total 22 different cities in which they had played games.

Even its antitrust lawsuit against the NFL went bad, for the USFL won only $1.00, trebled under antitrust laws to a whopping $3.00. Their lawyers did okay, though, because an antitrust victory is normally accompanied by an award of attorneys fees, so the USFL lawyers extricated $5.5 million from the NFL—after all, a $1.00 victory is still a win.

The written court opinions revealed the keys to the USFL failure, as the court was unimpressed with the USFL motives in moving to a head-to-head fall schedule. They brought their problems onto themselves, and in particular the court did not trust the USFL motives—was it simply trying to extort a merger from the NFL? How the league handled its court case was just an extension of how it managed its business—a series of blunders.

AFL out-hustles the NFL

The NFL has successfully staved off all meaningful competition, save for one trail blazing competitor, the American Football League. Formed in 1959 principally by Lamar Hunt, the AFL began league play in 1960 with eight teams, many of which were destined to become storied franchises of the NFL itself.

Although some of the teams had to play in high school stadiums, the league did manage to land a humble television contract with ABC which, although it paid less than $2 million for the whole season, gave the fledgling league an air of credibility. The AFL stumbled through four seasons without folding, then nailed a $36 million television contract with NBC in 1964, going full tilt against the NFL and CBS. NBC cleverly scheduled games after key NFL contests on CBS, piggybacking onto the football-starved NFL audience. CBS and the NFL attempted to fight back, but it was too little too late. Even though they scheduled double headers of their own to counter the NBC audience, the nimble AFL had already moved on to its next trick: signing big name players for more money fast. They scored a few good ones, but when New York Titans owner Sonny Werblin changed his team name to the Jets and dropped a record $427,000 on a brash country boy from Pennsylvania named Joe Willy Namath, the league aced the NFL for good. AFL games became entertaining, even great television with trench warfare among teams like the Raiders, Jets and Chiefs led by the likes of Lamonica and Namath, and by the spring of 1966 the NFL was talking merger. When Lamar Hunt, owner of the Kansas City Chiefs (once known as the Dallas Texans) secretly met the Cowboys' Tex Schramm in a Dallas airport lounge, the seeds were planted for a 26-point merger plan which would be consummated and announced on June 8, 1966.

But Lamar Hunt's contribution to the world of pro football was not over. Published accounts tell the story of Hunt's daughter and her remarkable "Super Ball," inspiring Hunt to change the NFL-AFL championship banner to the catchy "Super Bowl," not only altering the football landscape forever but launching a new American experience of nearly religious proportions.

The merger eventually worked for everyone concerned, but it likely could have been avoided had the NFL not been napping. The NFL learned, however, defeating all future comers, notably the USFL (blunder #12) and the WFL in years to come.

CHAPTER TEN:
The Mother of All Blunders

The top 10 all-time blunders, exercises in stupidity that clearly shape the sports world today. Perhaps because it has been around so long, or maybe as a function of its eroding fan base and other troubles, Major League Baseball scores seven of the top ten sports blunders, a daunting testament to Baseball's legacy, whatever history may prove it to be.

10 Messersmith vs. Baseball

Arrogance breeds contempt, and contempt induces failure.

Modern player free agency traces its roots to a dramatic shift in the balance of owner-player power that rocked the sports world just over two decades ago when a brash Los Angeles star blew a gaping hole in the Baseball reserve system. Dodger Andy Messersmith, joined by American Leaguer Dave McNally, defeated Major League Baseball with a stunning 1976 labor arbitration award. Their victory remains one of the most significant reasons that today's free-agent athletes, including those from other sports, do not remain trapped in a stranglehold of powerful owners from eras past.

Messersmith decided to challenge the reserve clause system after he came off a stellar 1974 season for a pennant winning Dodger team where he was 20-6 with a 2.59 ERA, deciding to play the 1975 season without a new

171

contract and testing the one-year renewal language of his just completed contract. His timing was good, for in 1975 Messersmith lead the National League in starts with 40, complete games (19), and shutouts at 7, all with fewest hits per nine innings at 6.8 and a sparkling 2.29 ERA. After 1975 Andy Messersmith went to war against Major League Baseball.

The powerful Baseball reserve clause had chained players to their owners forever, stymied courts and lawyers, and held free agency at bay for virtually a hundred years of Baseball. However, during much of Baseball's history, the clause itself was a phantasm. It was a fiction—it did not exist, even during the Ruth years and the 1927 Yankees, Ty Cobb, and Shoeless Joe. The feared "clause" never appeared in the original Major League Agreement at all; rather, it was only a system by custom stemming from 1899 when the National League encouraged member clubs to curb player defections to rival leagues. Restrictive language was purposefully used in the Uniform Players Contract in 1930, which was amended in 1947 to include a rather simplistic club renewal paragraph restricting player freedom.

Apparently no one read the words carefully for almost 30 years until Andy Messersmith stepped to the plate and took a rip at nearly a century of Baseball serfdom by arbitrating its literal meaning in 1976. Remarkably, the arbitrator read the feared reserve clause and found its literal meaning to require only a one-time one-year renewal—after which Messersmith and all others would, and always should have, become free agents. Messersmith had truly shocked the sports world when he used these ill-fated reserve clause words against the surprised owners: "...the club shall have the right by written notice to renew this contract for a period of one year upon the same terms..." Baseball's establishment argued the clause was in effect perpetual, for "each time the contract renewed, the one-time renewal should legally and logically be reactivated with it," thus generating an endless cycle.

The arbitrator said no, suggesting Baseball's argument ran afoul of additional language that required the club to pay the renewed player at least 75% of his prior salary. Extending this option to its logical conclusion, the arbitrator opined that a team literally would have the right to retain the player forever, with a 25% pay cut each year such that over time his salary would approach zero. Such fractured logic prompted the arbitrator to find that the renewal language as drafted was intended to be implemented only once.

With that the great reserve clause was no more, beginning a two-decade transfer of economic power to the once oppressed Boys of Summer, Autumn and even Winter, for over the next decade the federal courts would also inject free agency into the NFL and other leagues, spreading the right to various forms of freedom throughout pro sports. And from the owners' perspective, the collapse of the house of cards was so unnecessary the way it happened. The arrogance of the Baseball establishment had allowed those weak words to comprise the reserve clause for years, never thinking they would be challenged or overturned. But even those shallow words may have passed muster without the greed of the next clause calling for a 25% pay reduction each year into infinity—this was too much for the arbitrator to swallow, and it belied the intentions of the owners and the league.

This blunder would rank even higher but for the fact that free agency was inevitable eventually, given the attitudes of courts and labor unions alike, but the sheer shortsightedness of the owners and the way the reserve system collapsed deserves its top-10 ranking.

The 1919 Chicago Black Sox

The Black Sox scandal over the fixing of the 1919 World Series is fraught with blunders. Whatever players were actually involved blundered, as did Commissioner Landis when he booted out innocent players in a knee-jerk reaction, for on top of it all the accused players were actually cleared of chargers in court. Many of the participants never knew or even met each other; and most conspirators had no clue what the others were doing—so even the conspiracy seems to have been a blunder all its own. According to published reports, apparently the grand jury transcripts have been missing from the Cook County, Illinois, Criminal Courts Building, and the only record of the events are remaining newspaper accounts, which are plentiful.

There were many personal tragedies of the Black Sox episode, including that of Buck Weaver, one of the players acquitted in the scandal. Five months after his acquittal, Weaver approached Commissioner Landis who was upbeat and friendly, even offering Buck a chew of the commissioner's special tobacco. Buck felt good about himself. He had played all the games of the 1919 Series to the best of his ability; he had not taken a single dollar of dirty money; he had just been found not guilty of all charges; and on top of all that he was still one of the best, if not the best third baseman in all of Baseball.

Buck recounted to Landis how he had been approached by a gambler and was offered money for the fix, but Weaver had proudly rebuffed the intruder and played all the games straight. Instead of rewarding Weaver's integrity, though, Landis chided him for failing to stop the scheme or to report it to the authorities. But Weaver hadn't known enough to talk; he did not know who took money, or even if anyone did. Undaunted, the power-mad Landis banned the proud Weaver from Baseball for life, not to his face or by letter, but with this terse statement to the press: "Birds of a feather flock together. Men associating with gamblers and crooks could expect no leniency." Weaver worked for years to clear his name, even appealing to new commissioner Happy Chandler who eventually replaced Landis, and then to successor Ford Frick after that. But no one had the decency to right a human wrong, instead hanging Buck Weaver out to dry. More than thirty years later Buck was walking down a Chicago street on the south side when he suddenly dropped in pain, dead of a heart attack at age sixty-six. He probably died of grief—and if he didn't he had a right to.

Yes, the players, the gamblers, Commissioner Landis, all conspired to sell out Baseball. Two wrongs do not make a right, as they say, and so even Landis owes history, if not fans and players, an explanation—if only he were around to give one. In any event, the Chicago Black Sox episode changed Baseball forever, and even influences the game today—just ask Pete Rose, or ask the families of Shoeless Joe Jackson or the heartbroken Buck Weaver.

Cancellation of the 1994 World Series

After backpedaling for two decades while the players union rolled over Major League Baseball owners, the owners responded to 1994 labor problems by canceling the 1994 World Series.

Given all the labor strife at the time, one cannot conclude the Series would have taken place anyway, but by canceling it the owners pushed Baseball into a hole. This was significant, for Baseball has been battling ill will and negative perceptions for the better part of twenty years, much of it with the help of former union chief Marvin Miller, some of it due to their own actions. Not only did canceling the Series create a public relations nightmare, it took a negative spotlight off the recalcitrant players and shined it squarely on the owners.

Although not widely reported, this also had an impact upon Baseball licensing, for many of the licensees who pay big money for the right to sell merchandise with Baseball logos experienced financial hardship when the fall buying season was yanked out from under them. Most major retail stores do significant Christmas inventory buying during and around October each year. If sales are strong, they even do re-orders in November and December. When the Series was canceled, it sent financial reverberations throughout the marketplace, hurting the very people Baseball should court: large and small commercial enterprises that financially support Major League Baseball, its properties and related merchandise.

The timing could not have been worse, for Baseball has been losing support among young fans and buyers of merchandise as Baseball licensing revenues plummet. If Baseball were only experiencing a temporary lapse, perhaps such action would not have made the blunder list—or at least scored so highly on the list—but Baseball has made seven of the top 10 blunders, many of those in contemporary times, and it could ill afford another mishap. Canceling the Series was not necessary; fate would have intervened sooner of later—it either would have happened or not, anyway, and so the owners had no reason to make themselves look bad prematurely, if at all. And they certainly did not need to fire a missile at their merchandise manufacturers and other licensees.

Either way, the knee-jerk termination of the 1994 series was a mistake that still dampens fan support.

Flood vs. Kuhn

Curt Flood's celebrated antitrust case against Major League Baseball is often credited with opening the doors to free agency It did not. So far as setting legal precedent goes, the case accomplished very little. But it was the catalyst for two sports blunders, one of which officially makes our list.

On St. Patrick's Day in 1871, the National Association of Professional Baseball Players was organized, setting the stage for modern professional baseball. Curtis Charles Flood was born in 1938, and 18 years later he began his Major League career by signing on with the Cincinnati Reds for $4,000 per season. Two years later, just before the 1958 season, Flood was traded to the St. Louis Cardinals where he starred from 1958 to 1969. In his 12 years as a Cardinal, Flood compiled a cumulative batting average of .293, with six of those years at .301 or better. Flood played in three World Series, played totally errorless ball for the whole 1966 season and won the Golden Glove award seven times.

Although he was a perennial star, Flood never made more than $90,000 as a Cardinal, averaging only about $40,000 per season. Then, at the age of 31, the Cardinals suddenly traded Flood to the Philadelphia Phillies without prior notice to Flood and certainly without his consent. He asked the commissioner to make him a free agent so he could negotiate with other teams, and when the commissioner failed to intervene Flood filed an antitrust suit against Major League Baseball in January of 1970. Flood also refused to play for Philadelphia, sitting out the whole year despite an offered raise in pay to $100,000. After the 1970 season, Philadelphia sold its rights in Flood to the Washington Senators who signed him at $110,000 per year. Flood started the season, but played only until April 27, after which he walked off the field never to play Major League baseball again.

Flood decided to take on Major League Baseball, suing in federal court on the premise the club reserve system was a cooperative effort constituting a conspiracy to restrain trade in violation of the Sherman antitrust laws. This was a significant step, for Major League Baseball had already been exempted from antitrust laws by the United States Supreme Court in an illogical, bungled decision from 1922 (more on that at blunder #1). Flood's own blunder was more personal than profound, as he would have been better off taking his $100,000 from the Phillies instead of sitting out; rather, the key blunder was committed by the courts which refused to overturn the ridiculous decision from 1922 proclaiming that Baseball was not a business engaged in interstate commerce. Since it supposedly was not such a business, by definition it would not be subject to federal antitrust laws—hence the peculiar Baseball exemption.

Even if one were to dismiss the 1922 decision as an historical oddity born of archaic thinking (but we cannot let them off the hook so easily), the decision in the Flood case occurred in 1972, a time when the national character of the baseball business was in full tilt, complete with television money, sports marketing and all the trappings of a monolithic interstate enterprise. And the Flood case 1972 Supreme Court decision was accompanied by strong dissents from Justices Marshall and Brennan who stressed the illogic of such a charade. Essentially the majority argued that even though Baseball *was and is* a business in interstate commerce, Congress somehow should have intervened since 1922 to change the law, and because it did not, the Supreme Court was not about to reverse itself and now come to a rational decision—more or less admitting it was being stupid, but then blaming its own witless conclusion on the recalcitrance of Congress. Justices Brennan and Marshall, on the other hand, exposed the majority decision for what it was in their published dissent: "...an aberration confined to Baseball." Since no other major professional sports league is materially different from Baseball, and all are subject to antitrust laws, these periodic Supreme Court decisions go beyond blunders, they are a twentieth century sports law embarrassment.

Amateur Olympians

Athletes from many, if not virtually all countries, have benefited from subsidies, training assistance, or even outright government sponsorship for years. As a result, the Olympic Committee charter, which banned any competitor who "...received any financial rewards or material benefit in connection with his or her sports participation," served to work against American interests, keeping U.S. participants at a disadvantage as strict amateurs.

Supporters of the rule cited the purity of amateurism—why it was supposedly pure is not adequately explained—but even this lofty, but vague support was misplaced. Some historians attribute the amateurism precedent to a less than noble motive of the English upper classes who revived the Olympics in 1896, seeking to exclude the working class and allow participation by only the wealthy, non-working aristocracy. If such a theory is accurate, then all arguments of purity are wholly misguided.

As it came to pass, American adherence to amateurism hurt American competitors by often keeping the best athletes off the team, and causing a hardship for non-professionals who nonetheless required assistance for training and related purposes. When U.S. Olympic teams sank deeper and deeper, eventually losing even the basketball competition, authorities, fans and the media began to take note, denouncing such a falsely veneered rule as having no logical place in a modern world. It was unnecessary, just plain dumb, a blunder—and predicated on a false premise at that, for amateurism may have just been a means of discriminating against the working class in the first place.

Ueberroth's Baseball Collusion

Baseball owners have a history of playing hard ball, and not just on the field. Hall of Famer Jimmie Foxx won the triple crown in 1933 and was rewarded with a pay cut offer. Ralph Kiner led the National League in home runs for seven straight years, and after the last one he had his pay cut. "We finished last with you," explained Branch Rickey, "and we could have finished last without you."

Years later when the owners opened their books to the players' union in the 1980's their unique accounting talents became obvious. Many teams could show a loss, but still be making money for their owners hand over fist. Many of the shenanigans were made possible when owners also owned the stadium, parking facilities, concessions or TV rights. For example, Ted Turner, as owner of both the Atlanta Braves and superstation WTBS, has the power to manipulate how much the Braves charge for the sale of television rights to his own carrier. When league books were opened for scrutiny, it was reported that WTBS was paying the Braves only $1 million per year for TV rights at a time when the league average was a heftier $2.7 million.

When the players association continued to make significant headway in free agency following the Messersmith arbitration, the owners grew anxious. When Peter Ueberroth was elected commissioner in the 1980's, he and the owners attempted to address the problem by working together. After the 1985 season, Ueberroth convened a series of meetings with the owners on the economic danger of bidding wars for free agent players. Apparently the meetings were effective, as 26 of 46 free agents switched teams the year before, but only 4 of 32 free agents switched the year after—and none of the departing four were wanted by their home teams. Of the remaining 28 who did not switch, absolutely none received an single competing offer from another team. While all this was happening, or more accurately "not" happening, the rate of salary growth slowed dramatically.

But Major League Baseball had been exempt from antitrust conspiracy since 1922, so where was the blunder in all this? Couldn't the owners conspire all they wanted in such a pro-Baseball legal environment?

They could not, it was their own fault, and that was their mistake—and what a blunder it turned out to be, tracing its roots all the way back to star Dodger pitchers Sandy Koufax and Don Drysdale who, after a stellar 1965, conducted a unique joint hold-out in 1966 over a double salary dispute, leaving a bad taste in owner mouths. In response to the dangers of such joint negotiating, the owners later were able to preclude the practice in revisions to the collective bargaining agreement, resulting in this fateful clause:

The utilization or non-utilization of rights under this Article XVIII is an individual matter to be determined solely by each player and each club for his or its own benefit. Players shall not act in concert with other Players and Clubs shall not act in concert with other Clubs.

A careful reading of the above reveals the clause goes *both* ways. Just as the owners negotiated an end to joint player hold-outs, the players responded by inserted a similar prohibition against owner collusion. Did the owners later forget? Did they not understand it? Did they not care? Whatever the reason, the owners' collusion was attacked in a massive grievance arbitration conducted over five years and producing over 17,000 transcript pages. It also yielded a disastrous result for the owners with a 1994 financial award to the players of $73 million in lost salaries for 1986 and 1987. Big winners of over $1 million each included an array of stars such as Carlton Fisk, Jack Clark, Lance Parrish and Tom Seaver. The owners also committed $280 million to the aggrieved players to settle all claims for all years, a monstrous award—all stemming from a simple little clause that effectively negated part of Baseball's antitrust violation, and dramatically rocked the balance free agency in favor of the players.

Portland Passes Up Michael Jordan

What more can be said about Michael Jordan? Volumes have been and will continue to be written on the impact of one Mr. Jordan on the American sports scene. But was his fabulous career and the explosive success of the NBA born of a giant sports blunder?

MJ was born in Brooklyn, New York, on February 17, 1963, barely entering life in the pre-Kennedy assassination era. A svelte 6'6" and fiercely competitive, he was born, it seems, to play basketball. And so he did.

In a preview of his penchant for game altering heroics, Jordan hit the winning shot in the closing seconds of North Carolina's one-point victory over Georgetown to win the 1982 NCAA championship— as only a freshman. Two years later he was the college player of the year, leaving school as a junior to enter the NBA draft. The Chicago Bulls were waiting, but legend has it they really wanted seven-foot journeyman-type center Sam Bowie from Kentucky—a blunder poised and waiting—but Portland picked one slot ahead of the Bulls, however, and literally stole the blunder. The Portland Trail Blazers were enamored with Bowie's size, even though he did not possess the obvious tools of power, dominance and stamina required of NBA centers—in fact, he had missed most of two seasons at Kentucky with leg problems, and so they picked Sam Bowie ahead of Michael Jordan, leaving Jordan for the Bulls who obliged by snapping him up ahead of the rest of the crowd. Perhaps Portland was upset at missing all-world center Hakeem Olajuwon in the first pick of the same draft, for they lost the first pick on a coin toss with the Houston Rockets, and so they went after another big center—losing sight of Jordan?

No one could have predicted the extent of Jordan's NBA dominance, not only reinventing the NBA game, but changing all of American sports marketing in the process, but on the other hand Jordan was no surprise. Had MJ come out of nowhere, perhaps Portland's miscue could be dismissed as an unfortunate quirk of fate; but he was not a fluke, and Portland's uninspired draft completely changed the NBA for at least two decades—if not forever.

Imagine Jordan as a Portland Trail Blazer and Bowie in a Bulls uniform. First of all, Bowie bombed out due to injuries and a lack of inspiration, while Jordan's career made history. Would it all have happened with MJ in Portland?

Probably not. The Bulls would most certainly have struggled, but what about Portland? Trail Blazer fans would have been happy, and since they have had some decent teams from time to time, it is possible MJ could have brought them a championship and with Clyde Drexler and Kiki Vandeweghe hanging around, he probably would have. He would not have brought them three in a row, nor five and counting in the 1990's, however. And even with a degree of success, the Portland market was not the same as Chicago, and may not have impacted the whole NBA and sports marketing landscape in the way Jordan was launched in Chicago, a sprawling market with ravenous former Chicagoans spread around the country from Florida to Arizona to prime the frenzy as it crept national.

When we conclude the Bulls would not have been the same without Michael, there is little room for speculation. What may have happened to the Trail Blazers is highly speculative, but it is unlikely the Jordan mystique would have unfolded the same way in the great northwest. To begin, Portland never had the likes of coach Phil Jackson, a necessary ingredient to the type of perpetual success the Bulls enjoyed. It is a mystery to the author why Jackson has not received the greatest of credit for the Bulls' continual success. As a winning player, CBA coach, assistant coach and owner of five championship rings as head coach, he certainly knows the game of basketball. But even more significant is Jackson's knowledge of people, in particular basketball players. It is shortsighted, unfair, and just plain wrong to dismiss the Bulls' success as a function of the strong willed Jordan. No basketball team wins unless it is a functioning unit, with all players pulling their oars in the same direction, with enthusiasm, toward a common goal.

Every NBA franchise looks for a coach who not only can be the glue to keep a team together, but the mentor to egocentric superstars who often put their own glory ahead of their teammates individually and their team as a whole. In this age of multimillion dollar contracts, the players are prone to revolt, as they did in Orlando, for example, when they engineered the ouster of their former coach. Along comes Jackson, though, who not only creates a star-friendly environment that allows—probably even causes—Michael Jordan to flourish instead of rebel, he masterfully oils all the fragile working parts to the great team machine, even inspiring the historical malcontent Dennis Rodman to applaud Phil as the "coolest cat I've ever played for." Even if one prefers the most skeptical approach—that Jackson just went along for the Jordan ride—the argument falls short. In the NBA mediocre and even good coaches screw up games, teams and seasons all the time. It takes a great coach to not mess everything up. Jackson is. And he didn't.

Without Jackson and a reasonably inspired supporting cast supplied by the underrated Bulls GM Jerry Krause (Scottie Pippen, yes, but also an interchangeable group that led various teams to the top, from John Paxson to Steve Kerr to Rodman to Bill Cartwright to BJ Armstrong to Ron Harper and many others) the Portland Trail Blazers would have enjoyed success, but not perennial dominance. And Jordan himself would not have the same aura of mystique he enjoys now; and the NBA would not be the same without that mystique which generates $3 billion per year in licensed merchandise sales, not counting what Jordan does on his own outside a Bulls uniform, and certainly not counting all the television and ticket revenue from the NBA dynamo we know today.

Meanwhile, Sam Bowie in five seasons with Portland missed one whole year with a broken foot, and would play a total of 63 games collectively over three other years. In his one full year of playing, he would average just 10 points per game.

Red Sox Sell Babe Ruth

The Boston Red Sox knew what they were doing. They did not sell a Wally Pipp only to have him turn into Ty Cobb, Hank Aaron or Babe Ruth—they actually dumped the established pro Ruth for cash. If ever there was a "natural," it was Ruth, a pitcher, position player and the most feared of power hitters in his if not all eras.

There should be little debate whether shipping Ruth off to the rival Yankees was a prodigious blunder, but the issue is whether to rank such a move ahead or behind the Portland-Jordan blunder. The answer is almost a crap shoot, as great arguments could be made either way. The author, a Chicagoan, reluctantly votes Ruth barely ahead of Jordan on the blunder scale, but only because of history, not for any lack on Jordan's part.

In 1920 a mediocre New York Yankees ball club paid $20,500 to Babe Ruth, the original team superstar. Freshly acquired from the Boston Red

The house that Ruth built could have had a Boston address.

Sox in a financial deal (which helped the Red Sox in the short run), this was the Babe's first year as a pinstriper. The ignited Yankees went on to win three straight American League championships, plus the World Series (one of many to come) in 1923. Throughout the Roaring 20's, Ruth would rewrite baseball history wearing his Yankee uniform including, of course, his own personal records such as the 60 home runs for a 1927 Yankee club which may have been the most awesome baseball team ever to take the field. Overall, Ruth had eleven seasons in which he hit over 40 home runs, and he still owns the Yankee team record for homers with 659—more than Mattingly, Winfield and Maris *combined*. Ruth also hit for average, and he still owns the Yankee lifetime mark of .349 (he led the entire league at .378 in 1924), plus leading the team in slugging percentage at .711, a full 150 basis points above Mickey Mantle. The Yankees as a whole became what may have become the most dominant dynasty in all of team sports, extending more or less from Ruth's first year in 1920 until New York's World Series dominance ran out in 1964 after a run with superstar Mantle.

Jordan himself probably dominates games more than Ruth did, especially since a one-man wrecking crew can cause more havoc on a five-man basketball team than a baseball power hitter, but the Ruth blunder edges the Portland-Jordan fiasco because (a) the Bulls as a team have not yet matched the Yankee periods of domination (although the 72-win Bulls team may have been the best basketball team ever assembled) and (b) passing up a seasoned pro in Ruth was still a little dumber, and less speculative, than passing the rookie Jordan—but not by much.

The Jesse Owens Olympics

One individual's sports blunder is often the mirror image genius of another, just as Portland's miscue on Michael Jordan was an inspired windfall for the Bulls. The great American Jesse Owens and an entire race of athletes benefited from a cruelly motivated back-handed blunder, launching a new era in sports competition and racial dignity.

Adolph Hitler, villainous leader of Nazi Germany's Third Reich, played host to the world as 52 foreign nations participated in the 1936 Berlin Olympics. In retrospect it seems remarkable that Nazi Germany could have pulled the games off, but Hitler was no stranger to propaganda and manipulation, and given Germany's ability to BS the world even as it invaded Poland, a staged Olympics to show off Aryan supremacy should be no surprise.

Jesse Owens was the antithesis of Hitler's regime. As an African American—before that dignified label became popular—the "Negro" Jesse Owens was a young American athlete, unsupported by the state, who overcame many adversities to take on the fundamental premise of the Third Reich: white supremacy. That Hitler dared Owens with the whole world watching was by no means the greatest of Hitler's innumerable wicked blunders, but strictly as a sports blunder it earns extremely high marks. Jesse Owens was not an unknown quantity. The year before he had tied one world record and set three others in one day, so the Nazi regime was on notice regarding the ability and character of this down home, midwestern athlete from Ohio State University.

Jesse Owens was actually born James C. Owens, but acquired "Jesse" in school when the teacher heard him use his initials with his name, thus "J.C. Owens." Jesse proved to be a natural athlete, and by age 19 he had run a world record 100 yards in 9.4 seconds, a mark that stood for 21 years. Then, at age 22, he found himself in a hostile Germany, a target of Hitler's team of white runners bent on defeating not just Jesse, but the entire Black race.

There were twelve preliminary heats scheduled for the 100 meter dash, and Owens was not up until the very last one. Meanwhile, the Germans methodically marched their stars to the starting line (blocks were not then in use). The white American entry ran a 10.6 in the 100 meters, sandwiched by the Germans: Borchmeyer ran a 10.7 and Osendarp was in at 10.5. By the time of the last heat, the overflow crowd of 100,000 was energized with anticipation.

Owens did not disappoint as he exploded through the 100 meters in 10.3, tying both the Olympic and world records. Owens was described as a whirlwind, a black panther, even a black bullet. But these were only the preliminaries; Jesse could still be beaten in the finals. Jesse was up to the task in the second round of heats, beating his own time with a stunning 10.2 seconds which would have set new records but for a small tail wind disallowance. The German Borchmeyer and Jesse's Black teammate Ralph Metcalf (later to become a U.S. Congressman from Chicago) won their respective heats, but only at 10.5 seconds each. By now the entire world was watching and listening, and all of Berlin received reports over loudspeakers

planted throughout the city. Most importantly, Owens won over the appreciative, massive crowd, which grew generous in its admiration for the history unfolding before its eyes, discrediting Aryan propaganda and even Hitler himself.

Before it was all over, Owens would break or tie nine Olympic records at the Nazi games, and would win four gold medals: the 100 meters, 200 meters, long jump and the 400 meter relay. Of greater his-

Sprinter Jesse Owens won a grueling marathon for racial pride and American respect. (Corbis-Bettmann)

torical significance was the world credibility that Jesse Owens brought the Black race, symbolically showcasing the potential for all Black Americans. White promoters and team owners could no longer pretend to discount the Black athlete regardless of nationality, although it would be several more years before Jackie Robinson and others would begin to erase the color barriers at all levels. Nazi Germany had blundered, but the world had scored a watershed victory.

"Baseball is not a business..."

Over the last twenty-five years the strongest player union in professional sports has belonged to Major League Baseball, and for most of the Twentieth Century Baseball has been exempt from federal antitrust laws stemming from an illogical, almost suspect, U.S. Supreme Court decision in 1922. This is no coincidence.

The NFL, NBA and even NHL have lost important antitrust battles over the last thirty years. Baseball did not, for it was exempted by the decision in *Federal Baseball Club of Baltimore, Inc. v. National League of Professional Baseball Clubs, et al.* Over the years when aggrieved players such as Curt Flood made no headway attempting to change the exemption, they were forced to look elsewhere for help. As it happens, Flood himself hooked up with union chief Marvin Miller who backed Flood in his famous antitrust case against Baseball. But the most important aspect of Flood's case, which he lost, was what happened later. The Baseball union began attacking the Major Leagues through the federal labor laws, and they quickly found a receptive court system which Marvin Miller skillfully utilized for the next twenty-five years, knocking the owners back on their heels almost every time.

The *Federal Baseball* decision changed the Major Leagues for seventy-five years and counting, inviting Baseball to conspire to restrain trade with abandon, oppressing players for the better part of a century and setting the stage for the strongest player union in professional sports. The dominoes continued to fall, as the strong player union led to much labor strife and eventually even caused the cancellation of the 1994 World Series.

The decision qualifies as a blunder not only for its far reaching effect upon Baseball directly (and the other sports indirectly), but because of its sheer folly not only in 1922 when the decision came down, but at least two more times when the Supreme Court had a chance to rectify the wrong but chose not to, usually copping out and blaming Congress instead of itself. The crux of the decision's absurdity is that the Supreme Court originally decreed Baseball "not to be a business engaged in interstate commerce." It is widely believed the court found that Baseball was not a business at all, and although it comes close, the opinion stops just short of such a conclusion, focusing upon the equally absurd notion that conduct of Major League Baseball does not cross state lines—never mind that the whole essence of Baseball is to travel and perform from state to state, routinely logging tens of thousands of miles by air (or at one time by train) in so doing. Following is an excerpt from the actual Supreme Court decision, written by none other than the normally lucid jurist Oliver Wendell Holmes:

"The business is giving exhibitions of baseball, which are purely state affairs. It is true that in order to attain for these exhibitions the great popularity that they have achieved, competitions must be arranged between clubs from different cities and states. But the fact that in order to give the exhibitions the Leagues must induce free persons to cross state lines and must arrange and pay for their doing so is not enough to change the character of the business."

This is such a grotesque twist of logic that it defies explanation, especially considering the source. During the 1920's and even before, the trust busters aggressively attacked a number of American businesses conspiring to restrain trade, but along comes Baseball which even in 1922 was a substantial economic enterprise, and the court runs for cover. Even more remarkable was the same result in the Flood case in 1972 when Baseball, television, and merchandising were undergoing explosive economic expansion in almost perpetual interstate commerce.

History cannot explain this complete fall from logical grace, but one can attempt educated speculation based upon the history of Major League Baseball. The 1919 Black Sox scandal was fresh, especially when the illicit conspiracy was not discovered or penalized until the early 1920's, exactly when Holmes' opinion came down. Judge Kennesaw Mountain Landis had been recently installed as commissioner, Babe Ruth had just been sold to the Yankees, and powerful, wealthy owners ruled Baseball with iron clad control over the reserve clause (what there was of it) and other devices of oppression. All of this begs a relatively short list of heartfelt questions.

Did the Supreme Court suddenly lose its senses, trampling all semblance of reality and legal reasoning? Did Holmes and company take it upon themselves to "save" Major League Baseball, anointing themselves as nine de facto commissioners ready to save the sport for Baseball, country and personal glory? Or were they bought off?

Here's a guess. The powerful owners of eras past traveled in highly placed circles and no doubt had the ear of the Supreme Court justices. They probably did not pay them off (the owners most likely were too arrogant, if not simply cheapskates), though that cannot be totally ruled out, but it is logical to speculate they scared the court—intimidating the individual justices into believing they would destroy Baseball by any other ruling for, of course, the owners had to conspire by definition to cooperate in maintaining a league with common rules and objectives. Consider the importance of Baseball at the time: it defined America; no, it *was* America. Babe Ruth, Ty Cobb, Tinker to Evers to Chance. The Supreme Court justices did not want to be remembered by history as the murderers of Baseball in America. They were psyched out by the owners or, to borrow a contemporary sports term, they "choked," falling for owner propaganda hook, line and sinker and curve.

So there we have it, the biggest sports blunder of them all—a whopper of national proportions founded upon a completely illogical, laughable twist of logic that Congress and the rest of the country bought continually for seventy-five years. And here is the irony: it was the *Federal Baseball* decision that made the Baseball union so necessary, and consequently so powerful, all of which led to an all-out interstate war between millionaire owners and millionaire players, turning off fans, driving down attendance, crippling television revenues, and generally causing the demise of Baseball as the number one team sport in the country. So if the Holmes court wanted to avoid the scorn of history, it failed miserably, contributing to at least the partial demise of Baseball generations later—and positioning themselves as a laughing stock, a veritable national joke for their arrogant opinion on the non-business of Baseball, damn the state lines, full speed ahead toward their legacy of sports lunacy.

EPILOGUE:
Only History will Tell

Whether the stabbing of Monica Seles was a greater blunder than the Cubs losing Lou Brock, whether the 1963 enlargement of the strike zone was worse than the Herschel Walker trade, or even whether the famous Roger Maris asterisk belongs on the all-time blunder list at all, are certainly fair game for debate, and this is the essence of compiling any roster of the greatest sports blunders: debate, controversy, fun.

Nonetheless, the top twenty blunders as a whole are demonstrably more significant than the bottom twenty, while the sixty in the middle could be interchangeable depending upon individual criteria or points of view. Further, there no doubt are missing blunders which staunch fans will point out, and a couple of blunders are on the list to patronize the author's sense of humor, sense of history or both (see "Bull Durham's Wet Glove"). But all the blunders, in addition to being remarkably short sighted or just plain stupid, share a place in sports lore, if not history.

Many inane or objectionable acts routinely occur in sports, sometimes several per game, but if they had no particular effect upon their sport they are unlikely to receive "blunder" recognition. For example, Joe Namath's brash prediction of a Super Bowl victory over the Colts was, objectively speaking, a dumb thing to do—but it did not prevent a Jets victory, so it fails to officially appear on our dubious list. When Chicago Bull power forward Horace Grant dumped Chicago for Orlando it changed his career dramatically but had virtually no profound effects upon the NBA, the Bulls (who kept winning), or even the Orlando Magic (who didn't). It was perhaps a big mistake for him, but it has had no apparent historical significance.

The gambling and related problems of former Ohio State quarterback Art Schlister are renowned, but whatever Schlister may have accomplished in the NFL is highly speculative, and it is likely the one hurt most by his travails are Schlister himself. Even the bizarre contract hold-out of Mets player Marv Throneberry fails to qualify, for his descension into obscurity is barely even a trivia question, let alone an historical event.

If we emphasize playing errors, one could fill a blunder book per month, so on-field screw ups have not been counted. Golf, which is probably underrepresented, would perhaps top the blunder list if on-course mistakes counted. Consider the example of Sam Snead who coughed up one of the worst choke jobs in golf history at the U.S. Open in 1939. Snead needed only a par and a bogey on the last two holes for a victory over legend Byron Nelson who was already in the clubhouse with a 284. So what did he do? Sam three-putted from twenty feet for a bogey on the next to last hole. But he still had a chance, just needing a par on the last hole, a reasonably short 558-yard par five. He had already parred it three times in the tournament, requiring only one more for the automatic win.

Snead's blunder began in how he approached the 18th hole. He assumed he needed a birdie to win, and he never verified the score. Instead, he attacked the par-5 rather than play it safe for a par, which is all he would have wanted. The tee shot hit the left rough, then he knocked a two-wood against a sand bunker 110 yards from the green. Using an eight-iron instead of a wedge, he caught the lip of the bunker, and so he took another swing with the exact same club—plopping the ball into another bunker 40 yards out (at least he was sneaking up on the hole). Then he poked a bouncer barely onto the green for a fifty-foot putt which he almost made, the ball spinning as it rimmed out. The next putt, a three-footer, was left short for, altogether, one of the most inauspicious "eights" in pro tournament history.

Some peculiar stunts actually turned out smart. Track and field star Al

Oerter, who won an astonishing four consecutive Olympic gold medals in the discus from 1968 to 1980, believed in the art of psyching out opponents, and Oerter himself was reputed to be one of the best, beating better, younger athletes sometimes on his sheer will. One of the better track stories involved, as the author recalls, Olympic hammer throwers some 20+ years ago. The Americans went out to practice and observed where most of the ground dents occurred from prior throws, whereupon they walked beyond those indentations and made many more several feet beyond. After their practice, the Russians appeared and nearly destroyed themselves trying to hit the elusive distant marks.

Muhammad Ali's antics, for the most part, were pretty smart, too. Many of his opponents were beaten before entering the ring, as was Sonny Liston who had to endure an endless run of tortuous taunting before his first fight. Liston's performance became one of our blunders, demonstrating that one athlete's genius is often another's blunder which, if anything, is the essence of sports competition.

Blunders are the variety, the spice, if you will, flavoring sports agony and ecstasy — entertaining fans for whom hope springs eternal: if your team is bad, maybe the other guys will screw up. After all, the "game ain't over till it's over"— no?